WHEN LIFE GIVES

YOU LEMONS

WHEN LIFE GIVES YOU LEMONS

Remarkable Stories
of People Overcoming Adversity

Alex Tresniowski

McGraw-Hill

New York San Francisco Washington, D.C. Auckland Bogotá
Caracas Lisbon London Madrid Mexico City Milan
Montreal New Delhi San Juan Singapore
Sydney Tokyo Toronto

McGraw-Hill

A Division of The McGraw·Hill Companies

1 2 3 4 5 6 7 8 9 0   DOC/DOC   0 9 8 7 6 5 4 3 2 1 0

ISBN 0-07-135591-X

Printed and bound by R. R. Donnelley & Sons.

This publication is designed to provide accurate and authoritative information in regard to the subject matter covered. It is sold with the understanding
that the publisher is not engaged in rendering legal, accounting, or other professional service. If legal advice or other expert assistance is required, the services of a competent professional person should be sought.
> —*From a declaration of principles jointly adopted by a
> committee of the American Bar Association and a committee
> of publishers.*

McGraw-Hill books are available at special quantity discounts to use as pre-
miums and sales promotions, or for use in corporate training programs. For
more information, please write to the Director of Special Sales, Professional
Publishing, McGraw-Hill, Two Penn Plaza, New York, NY 10121-2298. Or
contact your local bookstore.

 This book is printed on recycled, acid-free paper containing a minimum of 50% recycled, de-inked fiber.

To Lorraine Stundis

Loveliest Rainey, you are my sunshine

CONTENTS

CONTENTS

Introduction

There is a story of a good and simple man—let's call him Harry—who failed at many things he tried to do. Harry was a decent but unexceptional student in school, and later one of his teachers would say that "nobody thought that he'd go far at all." As a young man, Harry invested his money in a zinc mine, even though he knew next to nothing about the mining business. Sure enough, the superintendent he hired turned out to be a crook, and Harry watched helplessly as the endeavor failed. "You would do better perhaps if you pitch me into the ash heap," he wrote his fiancée, "and pick someone with more sense and ability and not such a soft head." After that, he and a friend opened their own men's clothing store. But that, too, failed miserably, and Harry incurred enormous debts that took him 15 years to settle. "There goes Harry again," smirked an acquaintance after this latest debacle. Finally, an influential friend helped Harry get elected to the position of county judge, and it looked like his losing streak was over at last. But Harry was booted out of office after only one term, and quickly found himself unemployed again. "You don't want to marry [him]," Harry's future mother-in-law warned her daughter. "He is not going to make it anywhere."

She was, to say the least, mistaken. Despite the litany of failures that defined his early years, hard-luck Harry—as in Harry S Truman—wound up doing just fine for himself. He became the thirty-third President of the United States, and he will long be remembered as one of the best, most admirable presidents in American history. As for all the failures, setbacks, and bad breaks he endured—well, they helped forge him into the tough, resilient statesman he became. Truman proved that pluck and perseverance can turn the most hapless of failures into the most remarkable of successes.

And yet the lesson of Harry S Truman is hardly ever heeded. Rather than judge people by their efforts or integrity, we tend to judge them by whether they fail or succeed. Thus was Truman a dismal failure in the eyes of those who knew him—heck, he even believed it of himself. Those who fail are instantly stigmatized, branded losers by a society that worships the bottom line. Contemplating someone else's failure can make us squirm with discomfort, or exhale in relief that it wasn't we who failed. And if we do happen to fail, we feel ashamed, humiliated, ostracized from our friends and family. The Scarlett Letter in this society is "F."

The truth of the matter is that failure, as an experience, is vastly underrated. Sure, success is the name of the game, and nobody sets out to fail. But everybody does fail, and most people fail all the time. Even the best hitter who ever lived—Ted Williams—failed at his task roughly seven out of every ten times he came to bat. Failure is a fact of life in our challenging world; it's one of the precious things that bind us together as imperfect human beings. Put simply, failure has gotten a bum rap, particularly considering its extraordinary power to teach us things about ourselves. Adversity can be the very best thing to happen in your life.

●●●

That is the principle message of *When Life Gives You Lemons*, conveyed through the stories of the amazing people herein. People like Sally Jessy Raphael, the popular talk show host who may hold the world record for being fired from jobs. People like Dan Jansen, the speed skater who carried the mantle of failure for years before achieving his true destiny. People like Linda Fisher, the small-town baker who lost her livelihood only to find the greatest gift of all. Some are famous, some are not; many are wealthy, others just scraping by. None of them is a superhero or otherwise endowed with special powers. All of them have dreams and goals and fears and expectations, just like you and me. A few of them are athletes who measured success in points and seconds; several others are entrepreneurs, who see victory in terms of profits and sales.

But what they all have in common is the experience of failure. To varying degrees, they have seen their hopes dashed, their dreams wrecked, their worst fears realized. They have been to a destination no one wants to visit—a fascinating and fearful place that goes by the name Rock Bottom. Just how they wound up there is different in every story, and so, too, are the ways in which they responded once they were there. But, to a person, they all truly benefited from having faced adversity. The wisdom and insight they gained on their journeys are what make their stories so remarkable.

What they discovered is that failure unleashes a strength and power that lies dormant in us all. Challenges and obstacles that we dread are, in fact, opportunities for growth. The things we learn about ourselves when disaster strikes give us the skills to bring about real and lasting happiness. What Sally Jessy and Dan and Linda discovered is that the conventional definition of failure doesn't begin to describe the positive changes it can effect. What they learned is that when life gives you lemons, it's up to you to make some lemonade.

● ● ●

There are no theorems or principles or rules in this book. No postulates or game plans or success exercises. This is a book of stories, plain and simple. After each story, there are a few "Tips for Tough Times," extracted from the hard-earned wisdom of the story's subject. But the real inspiration lies within the stories themselves. In each, there are moments of heartbreak and pain, of sadness and tragedy, of glory and exhilaration. In other words, each story is profoundly human. Sharing in the struggles and triumphs of the people in this book will, with any luck, inspire and motivate you in your own quest for success.

Which is not to say that this is some sort of handbook for people who fail. Adversity is the ordeal that links all the stories, but the lessons that they hold can be useful in any circumstance. Naturally, if you have confronted failure, or have struggled and suffered mightily, these stories will have particular relevance for you. But anyone who is looking for an edge in life will benefit from the unique perspective of the survivors in this book. Even if everything is going just swell, reading about these adventures can help make your life a richer, deeper experience.

Next, you'll meet the inspiring people who treated adversity like a pit stop on the road to happiness. People who faced soul-shaking failure and somehow turned it into life-affirming success. People who teetered on the edge of giving up, but somehow summoned the strength to persevere. People who hit rock bottom, only to bounce right back to the top. They are, in their own different and fascinating ways, testaments to the incredible resiliency of human beings—to the indefatigable spirit that resides inside us all.

Acknowlegments

Great big thanks go to Lorraine Stundis, for coming up with key ideas and brilliant suggestions that made this book happen, and for the kind of relentless support a writer dreams of having.

All the thanks in the world also go to Andrew Stuart at the Literary Group, the razor-sharp mind behind this book, and to Frank Weimann, simply the best there is in the business. Thanks as well to Carol Wallace, Jack Friedman, Susan Schindehette, and everyone else at *PEOPLE*, for always being in my corner; to Amy Musher, for her years of friendship and nurturing; to Betsy Brown at McGraw-Hill, for her graciousness and insight; and to Mark Apovian, for the golf tips.

Thank you, kindly, all of you who helped me tell these remarkable tales: Andrew Friedman, Carol Castaneda, Evan Morganstein, Dean Hutchinson, Bob Sawyer, Raymond Ridder, Wesley Maat, Rich Hul, Lee Steinberg, Bob Muh, Peter Raskin, Jim Loehr, and especially Robbie Motter and Ginger Hornberger.

Finally, my profound thanks to the amazing people in this book, who honored me by opening up their lives and sharing their struggles, enlightening me to levels of strength and courage I hadn't known and, I hope, lifting those who read their stories to new and magical heights.

Alex Tresniowski

WHEN LIFE GIVES YOU LEMONS

1 STANDING TALL

The Michael Ain Story

It is far better to dare mighty things, to win glorious triumphs even though checked by failure, than to take rank with those poor spirits who neither enjoy much nor suffer much because they live in a gray twilight that knows not victory nor defeat.

Teddy Roosevelt

The tools of his trade are chisels and saws and drills and graters with big, razor-sharp teeth. His special skills are strength, precision, and nerves of steel. His canvas is the human body. Michael Ain is an orthopedic surgeon at Johns Hopkins Hospital, and there he undertakes the rigorous challenge of sawing through bones, resetting hip joints, and banging on prosthetic limbs with heavy surgical mallets. Watching him operate is like watching a world-class mechanic tear apart a vintage sports car and put it back together. It is tough, dirty, often wrenching work, requiring great exertion and even greater stamina. Dr. Ain, 38, is one of the very best orthopedic surgeons in the country.

He is also only 4 feet, 3 inches tall.

Ain is one of only three physicians in the country who are dwarfs and, as far as anyone can tell, the only one who is a surgeon. His achievements would be admirable for a man of any height, but considering the obstacles that Ain faced, his status as an elite surgeon is truly extraordinary. To everyone, that is, except Michael Ain. He rarely thinks about his height, and the instant people get to know him, neither do they. His patients and colleagues see him simply as a bright, friendly, compassionate doctor who really, really loves to operate. "I like the physical nature of it, the challenge of it, the immediate gratification," says Ain, who also makes furniture in the basement of his Baltimore home. "Someone comes in with a broken leg, the next day it's fixed. A guy's back is crooked, and now it's not. I love that. I love working with my hands."

Perhaps the most amazing thing about Dr. Ain is that he very nearly did not get to become Dr. Ain. When he first decided he wanted to pursue a career in medicine, he sent out 30 applications to medical schools across the country. *And all 30 schools rejected him.* Most people in his position would have gotten the hint—pick another field, you're not cut out for medicine. Most people would have moved on to other endeavors and spared themselves any further embarrassment. But Michael Ain doesn't embarrass easily. "For good or bad, I'm like a little pit bull," he says. "When I want something, I go for it and just hang on." Countless failures and setbacks only increased his desire to prove people wrong, to follow his dream wherever it took him. The key was never letting someone else decide what he could or couldn't do. "Through it all I never lost confidence in myself," he says. "I lost confidence in other people, but never in myself. It never occurred to me that, 'Hey, maybe I can't do this.' There was only one job I wanted in my life, and this was it."

●●●

Ain was the first and only dwarf born in his family, but right from the start his mother and father made sure he never saw it as a handicap. "My parents never set limits for me," says Ain. "They told me that my size was not an issue. And that support was crucial for me." Growing up in a middle-class town in Long Island, New York, Ain did everything the rest of the kids did: he played baseball, soccer, street hockey, softball, even football. He was on the wrestling team, and he played basketball in the seventh grade. "I just never thought of myself as being short," he says. "So it never occurred to me that I couldn't play these sports. I just did whatever I wanted to do, and if I wasn't chosen to be on a team, it wasn't because I was short, it was because I didn't work hard enough or practice hard enough or prepare well enough. I never used my size as an excuse."

When Ain was 19 years old, he had an osteotomy, a difficult operation in which his bowed leg bones were broken and straightened. He was in a body cast for 3 months, and a leg cast for 6 weeks after that. He also got his first good look at the world of medicine. "I met some good doctors and I met some bad doctors," he says. "And I found the whole field interesting." An excellent student, Ain applied to six top colleges and got accepted by all of them; eventually he settled on prestigious Brown University. His father, an attorney, wanted him to go into law, but Ain decided he wanted to be a doctor, and in his senior year he sent out some 30 applications to medical schools. "I covered them all, from the top rung to the bottom rung," he recalls. "I thought I had all my *t*'s crossed and my *i*'s dotted. My grades were good, my MCATs were good, I was from an Ivy League school. I thought they would be begging me to come to their schools. In my mind I thought there were no obstacles."

After he sent out his 30 applications—on all of which he mentioned his size, as well as his belief that it made him a better candidate—Ain visited the dean of a nearby college for a mock interview, as a way to prepare for what he thought would be a slew of invitations to visit schools. The interview went smoothly, until the very end. "That's when the dean said, 'Michael, it was great meeting you, it was really wonderful, and you've done some amazing things. Oh, and by the way, you will never, ever become a doctor. You should look for something else to do.' "

Ain never saw it coming. "I was absolutely floored," he says. "Devastated. It came out of nowhere. That was the very first inkling I ever had that my height would be an issue in getting into medical school. I was like, 'You're joking, right? Why? Why can't I be a doctor?' " The dean was blunt: He told Ain that he simply could not perform the functions of a doctor, given his size. Ain went for a second opinion, as it were, and set up another mock interview with a different dean. "And he said basically the same thing, that I would have a very hard time getting into any medical school." Then his father admitted that some friends he had consulted about helping Ain had told him the same thing. Great guy, that Michael, but a doctor? Not a chance. "At first I rationalized that maybe it was just one dean who had that opinion. Certainly not everyone would think that I had no chance. This bias against me can't be everywhere, I told myself. But it was."

Ain could have listened to the naysayers, but instead he blocked them out. He sat back and waited for his acceptance letters to trickle in. Soon the letters from medical schools started arriving, but they were all thin letters, instantly recognizable as rejections. "One by one, four by four, the thin little envelopes came back," says Ain, the memory still painful. "They didn't say why, they just said no. All along, even after the dean shot me down, I kept telling myself that there must be *someone* who wants me. But no one accepted me. Not one of the schools accepted me. Not one." All of his friends were being accepted by schools he had applied to, and some of them were clearly lesser students than Ain. But there it was, the indisputable truth—he had gone 0 for 30. "I said to myself, 'Listen, Michael, you have to do something to make yourself good enough to get accepted by one of these schools. You have to prove that you are what they're looking for.' It was like when I was a kid and didn't make a team. I just went back and worked harder and proved everyone wrong."

So Ain took two advance-level courses, published some research, got great grades, and sent out another 30 or so applications to medical schools. He took a job as a waiter to make money, and even worked briefly as an investment banker in New York City. But all the while he knew what he wanted to do, and he was sure that this time he would not be denied. Plan B? Ain had none. It was medical school or bust. So he sat back and waited for the next wave of letters to arrive.

One by one, they did. And one by one, he opened them. Thin little envelopes that he knew right away were rejections.

Actually, Ain did receive an invitation to interview at the Albany Medical College. It was not an acceptance, just a chance for the school's admissions officers to meet Ain face to face. The interview went beautifully, and Ain returned to his parent's Long Island home to wait for a call. None came. Days passed. Weeks passed. Still no word from Albany. By then, nearly every school had already rejected him. Why hadn't Albany at least sent a letter? Frustrated, Ain got on the phone and called the admissions department. "I said, 'Hey, what do you guys think of me? I haven't heard anything, what's going on?' And the guy on the phone said, 'Oh, didn't you hear. We accepted you.' "

Ain asked the man on the phone to repeat what he had just said. The man confirmed that Albany had accepted Michael Ain. Apparently the acceptance letter had been lost in the mail. The school was actually worried that Ain was rejecting *them*. Ain screamed out, pumped his fist, went a little crazy. Then he called his mother and told her the good news. She cried. He called his father, a judge, and had him pulled off the bench to come to the phone. His father told him he was extremely happy and extremely proud. Days later the acceptance letter from Albany arrived. Today, it is framed and hangs on the wall of his mother's home.

Ain was going to medical school after all. He had no doubts that he would do well there, and sure enough he did. He worked hard and received good grades. He made close friends, got along well with doctors, showed all the signs of becoming a success. He even selected a fairly advanced and specialized field to focus on: he wanted to become a pediatric neurosurgeon. He liked kids a lot, and, of course, he loved surgery. In medical school he and every other student got their first tastes of the operating room. Ain was instantly smitten, and never felt for a moment that he could not physically do the job. Heck, he had played nose guard against kids twice his size in high school. He could certainly hold his own in the OR with doctors who were taller. Ain applied to 14 neurosurgery programs, and received invitations for nine interviews. Conventional wisdom held that if you got more than six interviews, you were a lock to get in somewhere. Nine interviews? Ain was a sure thing. "And I went 0 for 9," he says. "Everywhere I went there was some guy who told me, 'You can't do it physically, surgery is not for you.' I'd say, 'Why can't I do it, I'm stronger than any candidate! Bring them out here and I'll bench press more than any of them! What exactly is it that I can't do?' But they kept insisting that I couldn't do it. It was the same garbage as before."

Ain dug in his heels and consoled himself with one thought: "There was no way any of these guys could be sure that I wasn't capable of surgery." He decided to apply for a general surgery internship, as a way to prove himself before reapplying to be a pediatric neurosurgeon. This time, he sent out 10 applications, some to good schools, some to mediocre programs, some to bottom-of-the-barrel institutions. "Guess what?" says Ain. "Zero for 10." His friends thought that Ain was joking when he told them he was shut out again. The dean's office at Albany summoned him to help him figure out what to do next. This time, Ain felt more than stunned. This time, he felt defeated. "I was angry," he recalls. "I never broke a door or punched a wall, but I was angry. It really rattled my confidence that I was going to be a surgeon. I sat there thinking, 'The bastards beat me, they finally beat me. They are not going to let me do what I want to do.' "

●●●

Ain looked at a map and picked out the place that was furthest away from Albany in the continental United States. That place was southern California. So he accepted a pediatrics residency at the University of California at Irvine, packed all his belongings into his tan 1984 Toyota Celica, and drove across the United States to get as far away as he could from the failures and defeats he had endured. The experience was therapeutic, and strengthened Ain's resolve to become a surgeon. After a while, he sent an application to the one place that had given him a chance before: Albany Medical College. He hadn't wanted to stay there before, but now his desire to become a surgeon was stronger than ever.

Never mind that dozens of professionals in the field had categorically told him he had no chance of ever operating on patients. Never mind that he had seen enough thin little envelopes to last a lifetime. He wanted to be a surgeon, and so he sent out yet another application.

Albany received 400 applications for four slots in their residency program for orthopedic surgery. They considered Ain's record, his grades, his determination. Above all, they considered his potential as a surgeon. They had given him a chance before, and he had made the most of it. Wouldn't he do the same if given the chance to operate? They called Ain with the good news: he was in. "Every time I think of what Albany did for me, I get a little emotional," says Ain. "Without them, I would be an investment banker."

Ain spent 5 years at Albany, honing his skills in the operating room. None of his patients complained, nothing bad ever happened. Indeed, performing surgery has never been much of a problem for Ain. "The mechanics of it came pretty easily to him," says Dr. Richard Hul, as assistant professor of orthopedics at Albany. "There were plenty of students who took a lot longer to get the hang of it. Yes, there were things he had to be aware of, and he was. His arms are shorter, he has less room for a sterile field. And he also has to address the concerns his patients may have. Most of the time, when I saw patients who were concerned, they would always realize very quickly that their concerns were not founded because Mike would gain their confidence by being a straight shooter. He would speak with authority, without being condescending. And he would quickly gain their trust." Hul says that Ain had to meet the same rigorous standards all the other students were held to. "If at any point along the way we felt that there was something he couldn't do, we would have had to say, 'Look, Mike, you can't handle this.' But he was never in any kind of situation like that during his training. There was never an instance when we had to say he couldn't do this or couldn't pass that. That just didn't happen with Mike."

Many smaller doctors stand on stools while operating; Ain just stands on bigger stools. Sure, he has to lean in a little more than doctors with longer arms, but that gives him more leverage to handle the heavy drills and chisels. And, yes, he has to get off his stool and go to the other side of the table rather than reach across a body, as many doctors do. "Big deal," says Ain. "That takes 30 seconds." When it comes to bedside manner, Ain is second to none, capable of putting his patients at ease, particularly his younger patients. "I think I am more sensitive to people's needs because I know what it means to be different," he explains. "Being a patient early in my life made me a better doctor. Having physicians not answer my questions, having them tell me what to do instead of consulting with me—I hated all of that stuff. I think I am a better doctor because I am short."

Ain accepted a fellowship at Johns Hopkins Hospital, one of the finest in the country. There, he has developed a national reputation, thanks to his decision to specialize in skeletal dysplasia, the severe bone conditions that often affect dwarfs. He didn't want to go that way, didn't want to let his height play any role in his choice of specialty. But then a fellow doctor told him about a magazine article he had read. It concerned a couple with a daughter who was a dwarf. The couple despaired for their daughter's future until they met a doctor who was a dwarf, a doctor who convinced them that their daughter could do anything she wanted. Ain recognized the doctor in the article—that doctor was Michael

Ain. "I'm not a very religious person, but I guess you could say that was a calling for me," he says. "I saw the impact I could have on people's lives, and I decided this was what I was meant to do. Patients need to be able to have hope, to have someone who understands them, who can be sympathetic. They need to have someone they can talk to. And I wanted to be that person. Plus, the parents look at me and say, 'If he can do it, then maybe my child can do it. Maybe my child can do anything.' "

Today about 30 percent of his practice is spent helping people with skeletal dysplasia, and patients come to see him from all over the world. His calendar is booked months in advance. The clinic where he works has one counter built to his height, and an x-ray view box set a few feet lower than the rest. They seem like small concessions considering Ain's position as a national leader in his field. And considering the hundreds of people he helps, both physically and emotionally. Hundreds of people who would have one less reason to be hopeful had Ain listened when everyone told him no.

That is the principle lesson that Ain, a reluctant role model, feels his story imparts. "Without getting corny, there is a quote I used a lot in high school," says Ain, who is happily married to Valerie, a part-time nurse (they have a daughter, Alexa, and another child on the way). "It's by Teddy Roosevelt. He said: 'It is far better to dare mighty things, to win glorious triumphs even though checked by failure, than to take rank with those poor spirits who neither enjoy much nor suffer much because they live in a gray twilight that knows not victory nor defeat.' Hopefully, I live by that."

Ain has certainly dared mighty things and won glorious triumphs, refusing to let the fear of failure condemn him to that awful gray twilight. "Nor did he ever allow his setbacks to make him bitter," says Dr. Hul. "Many people hold grudges, but he didn't do that. He just used his setbacks as motivation to prove people wrong." "To this day," says Ain, "if I want to do something, I just go out and do it. And if I fail, I fail. Failure is not the worst thing that can happen, you know. My father always told me, 'Wouldn't it be horrible if 20 years from now you sat around saying, 'What if?' I am 38 years old and I don't have any 'What if's. Failing at this or getting cut at that, or not getting in somewhere right away—those were all tough things. But saying, 'What if?' That would have been much, much worse."

TIPS FOR TOUGH TIMES

The Michael Ain Story

Because a fellow has failed once or twice, or a dozen times, you don't want to set him down as a failure till he's dead or loses his courage—and that's the same thing.

George Horace Lorimer

Thirty applications sent, 30 rejections returned—it was the kind of abysmal failure that could have easily ended Michael Ain's dream to go to medical school. After all, it wasn't that his grades were poor or that his candidacy was otherwise flawed. The obstacle was simply his size—or, more accurately, people's perceptions that his size would prevent him from becoming a good doctor. And it wasn't just one or two admissions deans who felt this way: it was 30 out of 30, a clean sweep. Who could have blamed Ain for believing the obstacle to be intractable and for settling on a career as an investment banker?

One person: Michael Ain himself. His early hardships in life—undergoing a grueling operation at a young age, playing competitive sports against athletes twice his size—had instilled in him a never-say-die approach to achieving his goals. More importantly, he learned early on not to use his size as an excuse, but rather to outwork everyone until he leveled the playing field. And so, when he got 30 rejections in *the mail, he responded by making himself a better candidate—and he eventually succeeded. Overcoming those early setbacks on his path to becoming a surgeon has, in turn, made him a better doctor.*

1. **Don't Look for Easy Excuses** Ain's parents never let him use his size as an excuse for failing, and that lesson turned out to be one of the most important he ever learned. When 30 out of 30 medical schools rejected him, he didn't say, "Well, the world is against me and I'll never make it," or, "I can't change how tall I am, so what chance do I have?" Instead, he realized that if he couldn't change his size, perhaps he could change people's minds—and he did. *Excuses are incapacitating— a convenient way for us to take responsibility out of our own hands and, worse, to stop trying.*

2. **Don't Just Keep Trying, Try Harder** People snickered when young Michael Ain tried out for his high school basketball team, and he could have handled the ridicule in two different ways: he could have played it safe and put away his sneakers, or he could have worked relentlessly to improve his skills and make himself a more appealing player. He did the latter. Thus, when 30 rejections flooded his mailbox, he instantly decided to make himself a better candidate for the next go-around. *Ain used failure as motivation to improve himself, not as a reason to feel bitter and defeated.*

3. Don't Let Fear of Humiliation Stop You Michael Ain's pursuit of his dreams left him wide open for potshots and ridicule. And while his exposure was extraordinary—he was the only short person among hundreds of prospective doctors—anyone who dreams big dreams invites a certain measure of scorn and skepticism. But Ain realized that the funny looks and hurtful comments were far, far easier to endure than the prospect of not trying at all. Ain had the courage to keep plugging away, because he dreaded the consequences of giving up. *Don't ever let someone else's doubts and insecurities decide your fate for you; humiliation is the price you pay for sticking your neck out high above the crowd.*

2 UNSTOPPABLE

The Sally Jessy Raphael Story

A great deal of success is being prepared. The rest is just outlasting everybody else.

Sally Jessy Raphael

Eighteen times. Most people experience it once or twice in their lives, or maybe a handful of times, or, heck, if they're really unlucky, maybe even a dozen times. But Sally Jessy Raphael went through it 18 times. That's right, one of the most successful broadcasters in the history of television was fired 18 *times*. That's 18 times that someone looked her in the eye and told her to pack her things and scram. "Was it discouraging? It was *terribly* discouraging," says the now iconic TV talk show host with the trademark red glasses and nurturing stage manner. "And after every single job I would tell myself that it was time to quit. 'That's it, I can't take it anymore, I'm doing something wrong, no one in the world will hire me.' Twice I even entered law school and told myself I was through with broadcasting."

Sally Jessy, of course, is far from through with broadcasting. She is entering the seventeenth season of her pioneering syndicated daytime program, "The Sally Jessy Raphael Show," a daily morality play about hot-button issues that has thrived for nearly two decades as dozens of similar shows have crashed and burned.

She has logged more hours on the air than all but a very few women in the industry; she was refining the now-ubiquitous talk show format well before Oprah hit it big; and she was already a seasoned pro before Rikki Lake was even born.

She is, quite simply, one of the most well known and enduring on-air personalities of the last century. And all because she learned how to manage one thing—failure. "I just did some math on my career," she says from her invitingly warm and pillow-filled office in midtown Manhattan. "From the day I got serious about being a broadcaster to the day I got my first good-paying job, it was 25 years. That's 25 *years* before I could support myself and my family, before my income got past the poverty line. Today I interview a lot of young performers, a lot of rock stars and DJs, and they always say, 'You know, I really worked hard to get this job.' And they are maybe 19 years old! It turns out they worked a year or two. And, of course, when I hear that, I smile."

Smiling is what got Sally Jessy through the lean years—or, rather, the lean quarter century. With the exception of some brief spells of self-pity after her firings, she never gave up hope of making it in the business, never doubted that she had what it takes, never got bitter about her setbacks. She stuck with her dream long after most reasonable people would have taken the hint, and she suffered through great hardships and sacrifice to get where she is today. She and her family lived out of a car and survived on crackers and ketchup. She was flat broke many times, and went on food stamps when things were particularly bleak. She saw women with far less experience and savvy get promoted ahead of her, simply because their hair was blonder and wavier. She tried out for 142 commercial voice-overs—*and never landed a single one.* Heck, she was already in her late 40s before she earned enough money to buy her first new car. Sally Jessy Raphael had every reason to abandon her goal and get on with her life, and yet somehow she persevered, the very embodiment of pluck and persistence in a business that eats weak-willed pretenders for lunch.

What was it that allowed her to endure? Unwavering optimism? Incredible confidence? Sheer naïveté? In fact, there were many reasons why Sally Jessy never bailed out on her dream, but chief among them was the simple notion that there was nothing else she wanted to do. Once she realized that, it was only a matter of waiting for the world to catch up. "I honestly, really believe that if you hold on to something long enough, way beyond when everyone tells you to let go, that somehow or another it will work out," she says. "A great deal of success is being prepared. The rest is just outlasting everybody else."

●●●

There were plenty of obstacles along the way, plenty of chances for Sally Jessy to pack up and turn around. But giving up was not the way her loving parents taught her to live. Her mother was a talented painter who doted on her, and her father was a dreamer with a distinct sense of style and adventure. They always encouraged their daughter to become whatever she wanted to be, and when they saw she had an interest in the arts, they made sure she got the education she needed. "My mother was really indulgent and said, 'Whatever it is you're going to do, let's get going,' " remembers Sally Jessy. "I had a heck of a lot of lessons. Fencing lessons, tap dancing, you name it. My mother hauled me around everywhere, to the Philharmonic, to museums, trying to make sure that I was well-rounded—that I was ready." When little Sally Jessy was young she would lay in the dark at night and listen to

Jean Shepherd, the legendary storyteller, weaving whimsical tales on the radio. After that, she was hooked. "I didn't know specifically what I wanted to do," she says. "But I knew that I wanted to be a performer, and I knew that I wanted to be famous."

She was only 14 years old when she made it on the air. Her first broadcasting job: reading the junior high news on WFAS radio in White Plains, not far from where she was raised in Westchester County, New York. Four years later, she found a husband and had two daughters, Allison and Andrea. Sally Jessy moved her new clan to San Juan, Puerto Rico—where she had lived with her family when she was 12—and she took a job reading the news for a local radio station. On top of that, she worked as a stringer for a news service, reporting from whichever Caribbean Island happened to be in political flux. "I spoke Spanish and I was willing to work for nothing, which was basically what stringers got," she says. "I went to Haiti, to Guatemala, to wherever people were killing each other, and I'd wait around until they were ready to put me on camera." The job, she says, "could really wear you out. You could wait out a whole war on a stool in some dingy bar. You spend three weeks in some country and finally you're standing on the runway and you get your 60-second spot, which they'll later trim to 30 seconds. And for the rest of the week you're in a bar swapping stories with other guys who are doing as badly as you are. Being a stringer loses its glamour pretty quickly, and when you're a mother with children, it *really* loses its glamour."

The job also presented Sally Jessy with her first formidable roadblock: Her husband and his family did not want her to work. "They didn't believe in my career," she says. "They thought I wouldn't be a good wife. Maybe his parents felt that it's not necessary for a wife to go out and do that, that maybe I should be home entertaining his friends." After two children and 5 years of marriage, she had a difficult choice to make—her husband or her career. "In those days, I think 99 percent of women would have chosen to stay. They would think, 'Gee, he's a nice person, he's well-to-do, he's funny, you don't hate him, you have two children, he doesn't beat you—what the hell am I looking for? Forget whatever little dream you have and be a good wife.' I think 99 percent of women would have said that."

Sally Jessy, part of the other 1 percent of women, amicably split from her husband and kept on chasing her dream. Two years later, a man named Karl Soderlund hired her to work at the San Juan radio station where he was an advertising salesperson. She hosted a call-in show from 1:00 a.m. to 6:00 a.m., for the princely sum of $275 a week. It was the most fateful job among the many that would follow. She and Karl fell in love and got married, and he would prove to be the most supportive husband a wife could ask for. "Every woman who wants a career should have someone like Karl," she says. "He was never threatened, never showed one iota of machismo. He simply said, 'This is the lady I love, and she has the potential to make 10 times more money than I could ever make. Let's go and do it.' He made all the traveling from job to job possible." In one city, Karl took a job as a waiter to make ends meet. In another, he worked as a night watchman at a hotel. "Somebody had to make money to keep things going, and so he took all these jobs along the way," says Sally Jessy. "And he never, not once, said, 'Maybe you should give up and look for something else.' He was just the most supportive man you could imagine."

He had to be, considering how slow her ascent would turn out to be. Over the next two decades, she went from job to job, from city to city, moving to whatever station would have her—nearly 20 in all. That willingness to relocate was one of the keys to her eventual success. "It's the nature of the radio business that you have to keep climbing the ladder," she says. "If you're working at a radio station that's ranked 135th in the nation, next you want to work somewhere that's ranked 125th. You have to keep moving up." Most women that she encountered, however, "never thought of themselves as mobile. They would think, 'I have kids, they have a school, we have a home, my husband is here, so I can't just pick up and move.' And I never thought that way. I always thought, 'I am a radio person, and I'll go where the jobs are.' My friends would say that I thought like a man, and that is either a supreme insult for a feminist, or some kind of sick compliment."

Such a transient lifestyle, however, came with a steep price. Sally Jessy not only had to uproot herself and her husband to chase her dream, but also had to move her young children from town to town and school to school. "One of my daughters was in 11 schools, and some people would say that's child abuse," she says. "But she would say that she had the opportunity to meet a lot of different people and really see the country."

Sally Jessy's relentlessly upbeat attitude made it easier on her family. She chose to view her difficult journey as a challenging adventure. "We always made everything a positive experience," she says. "When it came time to move, we had these stories we would tell the kids. Stories like, 'Look, it's so boring in Miami. Why don't we study Civil War battlefields? They happen to be on the way up north to where my next job is.' And the kids would buy it, up to a certain age."

Sally Jessy and Karl and the children racked up a lot of highway miles that way. At first they traveled in a clunker of a

Volkswagon, with one red fender and one black fender and a body that was a third color. Then they upgraded to a used Mercedes, roomy enough to fit the whole family but prone to noisy break-downs. Some nights they would stay in sleazy motels; other nights they would sleep in the car. So short on money that they could buy either gas or food but not both, they sometimes had to make do with crackers and packets of ketchup. At one point, they even went on food stamps. "What kept us going was one simple word—hope," Sally Jessy explains. "We always believed in ourselves, always had hope that this way of living would end. There was always someone telling us, 'Call me tomorrow and I'll let you know.' There was always that tomorrow, and always a reason to hope."

●●●

Still, Sally Jessy's faith in herself was tested, time and again. She took all sorts of jobs in the industry—24 in all. She worked on one show as a puppeteer, and hosted a cooking show even though she couldn't cook. She was a street reporter, a theater critic, a rock DJ, a news anchorperson. She showed up for one job at a Hartford radio station and saw bullet holes in the station's window. Not a single one of the jobs lasted longer than 18 months.

Most of them ended with her male boss calling her in to break the bad news: sorry, kid, you're fired. "The weird thing is that nobody ever says, 'You're lousy and that's why we're letting you go.' They always have some reason for it—we lost a sponsor, we're trying something different. And so you live in this world of being constantly rejected and not knowing why. You go home and you go over every little thing you did, everything said at the firing meeting, and you try to figure out why you were fired. You say, 'If only I had done that differently,' or 'That thing I said to my boss in the elevator—that's what got me fired.' You torture yourself that way, over and over again."

Eventually, Sally Jessy figured out a reason why she was being fired. "It boils down to one word: pretty," she says. "That's the only word that counts when it comes to women in the TV industry. It was true when I was coming up, and it's still true today. Prettiness is the coin of the realm. Just look at the 6:00 news anywhere. You'll never see a female reporter who looks like the old men on the show. I was always having to watch women who were not only less qualified than me but prettier than me succeed while I was left behind." On one TV anchor job, low ratings convinced Sally Jessy's bosses that she would be more popular if only she changed her hair. "Every time the ratings came in, I would get a makeover," she recalls. "They made over my clothes, my hair, my face, this and that. To be immodest, I thought I was the best street reporter they had, but no one ever said anything about how I read the news or handled assignments. It was all about my looks." That particular job lasted 9 months.

The first five times that she was fired, Sally Jessy chalked it up to youth and inexperience—to paying her dues. After that, the rejections began to sting. "I had friends who were making it, and friends who were quitting the business and moving on to better careers," she says. "And here I was, getting fired over and over again. It was painful, very painful, each and every time." After a while, the days after a firing were devoted to a familiar ritual. "My husband used to say, 'Sally, you're going to be allowed 3 days to feel sorry for yourself. Put on the Judy Garland records, here's a box of chocolates, and take this bottle of gin if you think you need it. So go in the bedroom, close the drapes, and cry your little heart out.' And then, after a couple of days, it was 'Pity party over! We need an income, you don't have a choice, so let's go!' " Two or 3 days, it turned out, was all the time Sally Jessy ever needed to recharge her batteries. "After that," she says, "it becomes very boring feeling sorry for yourself."

And then, always, she picked herself up, dusted herself off, stashed away the Judy Garland records, and cranked up the crummy old Mercedes once again. It was sheer determination that kept her moving forward, even when she had every excuse in the world to stop. At one point, she was flat broke and desperate for a paycheck when she was hired for a job in Hartford, Connecticut. The station manager there agreed to give her an advance on her salary, and so Sally Jessy and her merry gang climbed into their trusty car for the ride to Hartford. It wheezed and sputtered and made familiar noises, just as it had the many times they'd had to pull over and poke around under the hood. "Fortunately Karl is good with cars," says Sally Jessy. "He kept patching up the Mercedes, and it would die, and he would patch it up again." But then, one and a half miles away from the Hartford radio station, the Mercedes gave out once and for all. "And so we gathered up all our things and walked the final mile and a half to the station," she recalls. "A mile and a half, and all of us there, on the side of the road, lugging all our worldly possessions. But we had a check to pick up, and that would keep us going." Sally Jessy pauses to reflect on that remarkable day. "There have been many moments in my life," she says, "that were right out of a movie."

There were also scenes of great sadness, such as the day in 1979 when Sally Jessy's beloved mother passed away, after suffering a stroke. "She died relatively young, in a charity hospital," she says. "She was extremely important to me, and it was ghastly to see her in the hospital with a thousand tubes sticking out of her." Toward the end, Sally Jessy was pulled away from her bedside vigil by the chance to do a commercial that paid $200. "We desperately needed the money, so I took the job," she says. "And so I was standing on a dock filming this thing, and I see Karl walking up to me, and I knew right away that my mother had died. For months and months I had been unemployed, and the one moment when I took this job, she passed away. I guess life doesn't always go the way you want it to go." It was the kind of setback that might have made her bitter, that could have soured her on her dream once and for all. But Sally Jessy simply never stopped feeling optimistic. "Even then, during that terrible time, I was full of hope," she says. "I still believed that something big was about to happen."

●●●

And while she had believed that for over two decades, this time Sally Jessy was right. Not long after her mother died, she was hired to host an advice show on Talknet, a radio network sponsored by NBC. "I think my salary then was something like $40,000 a year, which to me was simply enormous, a *fortune*," she says. "And from the day I got that job to this very day, I have earned a living in the business." After so many unsuccessful stints and callous dismissals, she had finally found a venue where her natural warmth and biting wit added up to a winning formula. She did the radio show for 6 years, and midway through her stay there got the chance to host her own TV show as well. "The Sally Jessy Raphael Show" debuted on October 17, 1983, and, after some first-season jitters, emerged as a solid syndicated hit. Years later, plenty of women would get the chance to host their own issue-oriented TV shows, but back then, Sally Jessy was a pioneer in the genre. In 1989, she won an Emmy for Outstanding Daytime Talk Show Host.

The next year she bought her very first new car, a Toyota.

Sally Jessy Raphael had made it, just as she knew she would. Certainly, she never thought that it would take as long as it did, but, hey, she figured, that's life, and besides, what choice did she have? All she ever wanted to do was be in broadcasting, and nothing—absolutely nothing—was going to stop her from living that dream. Perhaps the most remarkable thing about her long climb to the top is that she never panicked in the face of constant failure and frustration. She never allowed setbacks to disillusion her, never turned a firing into a reason to stay bitter. She was, throughout her 25-year ordeal, poised and ever ready to seize her big chance once it arrived. Sally Jessy stuck around, and let the world catch up with her. "I look at old tapes of me and, aside from some age lines, I don't think I have changed one iota," she says. "My style of broadcasting is exactly the same now as it was then. What I see is a person who pretty much stayed the same person they always were."

If there is one lesson that Sally Jessy learned from her experiences with failure, it is that no matter how crushing the setback, the dream of victory should remain intact. "You have to imagine success along the way," she explains. "You have to see yourself sitting in front of the camera. You have to imagine just what that camera looks like, what the set looks like, the color of the walls, everything. And you have to make that image very detailed and specific, so that you never go to bed without watching yourself do what you want to do."

Driving in that clunky Mercedes and staying in sleazy motel rooms, Sally Jessy Raphael imagined a finer life. "In particular, I imagined the new house I would live in. I imagined the house and everything in it—it had to be big, and it had to be old money, not new money. And it had to be very gothic, with a big music room I imagined myself walking around in. I imagined every single detail of this beautiful house of my dreams."

Two years ago, Sally Jessy and her husband Karl moved into that dream house in upstate New York. It took a while to get there—a lifetime to be precise. But there they are, full of cheer and happy thoughts. "I've been in this business for 43 years now," Sally Jessy says. "And I'm still working, still going strong, still living the life I want to live. What more could I ask for?"

And she hasn't been fired in a long, long time.

TIPS FOR TOUGH TIMES

The Sally Jessy Raphael Story

Our greatest glory is not in never falling, but in rising every time we fall.

Confucius

Getting fired 18 times can't be good for the ego. In fact, Sally Jessy Raphael often felt like she didn't belong in show business, despite her lifelong dream to make it as a broadcaster. Everyone feels like a failure sometimes, but not everyone can shake off those feelings before they become crippling. How someone reacts to failure defines their character—not the failure itself. Sally Jessy's "pity parties" never lasted longer than a day or two, and then it was back to chasing her dream in her beat-up, broken-down car.

Nor did Sally Jessy ever let anyone besides her husband see her when she was down. To the world, she always presented herself as a winner: positive, professional, and just a tiny break away from hitting it big. She kept on doing what her heart told her to do, and waited patiently for the world to catch up. Or as she put it, a big part of success is simply "outlasting everyone else."

1. **Don't Wallow in Self-Pity—Nobody Cares** It's human nature to feel wounded after a tough defeat, and there's no sense in denying those feelings. Everyone feels the sting of

failure, the ego-bruising sadness of coming up short. But Sally Jessy never wallowed in those feelings for too long. She faced her failures head on, regrouped quickly, and set out tilting at windmills once again. *Feeling too sorry for yourself not only makes you a guaranteed failure, but a boring failure at that.*

2. **Trust in Your Dream Through Thick and Thin** The key to Sally Jessy's resiliency was her unwavering passion. She knew in her heart that broadcasting was what she wanted to do, and so she never stopped believing in herself. She even sacrificed a marriage to keep pursuing her dream. That sort of passion makes all the blood and sweat and tears a lot easier to endure. *Be sure that you believe in your goal with every fiber of your being—and once you're sure, trust that you are on the path you were meant to travel.*

3. **Act Like a Winner and the World Will Catch Up to You** Perhaps the most devastating fallout of failure is allowing it to make you feel spiteful and embittered. Getting up off the ground is harder if your hands are gnarled up into angry fists. Failure can create a defeatist attitude, which leads people to expect the worst and promptly sabotage themselves. But Sally Jessy was always thoroughly professional, job after job after job. She gave herself the chance to succeed at every step along the way. *Even in the face of agonizing defeat, don't ever believe you are anything less than a winner-in-waiting.*

3 FRANKLY SPEAKING

The Barry Potekin Story

The first rule of war is audacity. Don't train to survive, train to win!

Barry Potekin

One plain bagel and a lousy cup of coffee. That was all that Barry Potekin, big-time gold and silver trader, could afford to buy. Actually, he didn't even have enough money to buy that sumptuous breakfast himself. He was sitting with his father, Irving, in a Bagel Nosh on Chicago's Rush Street, and *together* they could only scrape up 80 cents, enough for one plain bagel and a lousy cup of coffee. "So we each took half a bagel and we pushed the coffee back and forth," remembers Potekin, 54. "I took a sip, he took a sip, I took a sip. And my dad—you could cut off his finger and he wouldn't cry—all of a sudden he starts bawling like a baby and he says, 'Son, look what we did, we ruined our lives.' "

It was difficult for Potekin to see his father so distraught. This was the strong and stoic man he had looked up to, and here he was, overcome by sadness and desperation. But Potekin also knew that his father was being kind when he said "*we* ruined our lives." In fact, it was Barry alone who was responsible for the mess they were in. Only a few months ago he had been a wildly successful commodities trader, working the gold and silver markets with a literal Midas touch. He made millions for himself, bought a big mansion, and picked out a brand new Cadillac every year. So sure of his market prowess was Potekin that he even agreed to invest his parents' considerable retirement fund. "I was on this wild ride that as far as I knew had no end," says Potekin. "Plus I thought I was the smartest guy in the world."

Then, in the space of a few short weeks, Potekin lost it all. The mansion. The cars. All his money. All his parents' money. All of it, everything—gone. "I went from living in a mansion to sleeping on a friend's couch," says Potekin. "I told him I'd be leaving in a week and I stayed for 10 months. I mean, I was absolutely wiped out. Total devastation."

Today, sitting in his sprawling Chicago home, surrounded by the spoils of his *second* improbable ride to the top, Potekin likens his dark days "to being lost in this terrible forest. I went in there a young man, and many years later I came out old, with gray hair and a beard. But I made it out, and that's the main thing. I made it out of that forest alive." What's more, the things that Potekin learned in the forest helped him secure the more lasting success he enjoys today. "Looking back, I would even say that that was the best thing that ever happened to me," he says. "It was a tremendous learning experience, and it brought out things in my character that I never knew existed."

●●●

The young Barry Potekin, the guy who thought he was smarter than everyone else, would never admit that there was any room for improvement. He was cocksure, a gunslinger, convinced he was destined for greatness—which, after all, was what his father always told him. An inventor who made a fortune with a sealed beam flashlight, Irving Potekin "was the all-time optimist, and the biggest supporter a kid could have," says his son. "If I did something stupid, he would look for the one tiny good thing in it. If I tripped over something, he would say, 'That was the greatest trip I ever saw.' He never blamed me for doing something wrong." From an early age, Potekin decided that his purpose in life was to make loads of money. To him, having money meant being able to do whatever he wanted. That was the goal, and no one could talk him out of it; in fact, he couldn't even fathom why everyone else didn't share his yearning for earnings.

When he was in his early 20s, someone handed him a book about commodities trading. Potekin started buying Swiss francs and Krugerands, and graduated to speculating on gold and silver contracts. "It was a risky business," he says, "but I was lucky enough to start trading in the mid-1970s, when inflation pushed the gold and silver markets through the roof." Of course, Potekin mistook good timing for vast intelligence. "That was maybe my biggest mistake, thinking I was so smart," he admits. "What I had to say meant everything, and what you had to tell me meant nothing at all." Bob Sawyer, a longtime friend and former business partner, says "there isn't a lazy, unmotivated bone in Barry's body. He's unbelievably quick and a very good salesman. But back in the beginning, Barry had a lot of rough edges. He still had a lot of learning to do."

Seven years after he bought his first gold coin for $100, Potekin had made his first million in the market. Then, after a period of slow and steady growth, the value of gold and silver exploded, and overnight Potekin went from rich to *filthy* rich. So rich that he paid cash for a 14-room, five-bathroom mansion near the lake in Chicago. So rich that he bought a brand new luxury car every year, whether he needed one or not. So rich that he ordered custom-made shirts by the dozen, at $100 a pop back when $100 was not chump change. One time, he visited his tailor to pick up his shirts and discovered that a small detail had been overlooked. "I told him to do it, and then I came back later and he still hadn't done it the way I wanted," says Potekin. "So I took the 12 shirts and threw them in the garbage right in front of him and said, 'Okay, let's start over.' I was so arrogant, so cocky. I was *way* over the top."

Potekin kept an apartment in Paris, and liked to fly back to Chicago just to throw parties for his pals. After one such New Year's Eve bash, he was rushing to make a flight back to Paris when he realized he had a kitchen full of dirty dishes. "You know what I did with all the dishes and pots and pans? I threw them away! Dozens of them, and I just threw them away because I didn't want to deal with them. And then I flew back to Paris." The sweet smell of success was so intoxicating, it even seduced Potekin's business-savvy father, who entrusted his son to handle his hefty retirement fund. "It was a lot of money and I was pretty conservative with most of it," says Barry. "But some of it I put in gold and silver."

Potekin also bought a ritzy condominium apartment in a luxury high-rise tower on Chicago's posh Sheridan Road. The day he moved in, the telephone rang as workers shuffled in and out with his brand new furniture. "It was a margin call, and they told me I had to come up with $50,000 in 20 minutes," says Potekin. "The movers were asking me where I wanted the sofa. I told them, 'Throw it out the damn window, I don't care! This is serious!' "

• • •

First the gold market collapsed, and then the bottom fell out of silver. "I never saw it coming," says Potekin. "Silver went from like $49 an ounce on a Monday to something like $11 five days later. It was plummeting so fast you couldn't get out. I got caught in a big way." Day after day, Potekin had to come up with money to pay off contracts, and wound up dipping into his parents' investments, certain that he would repay them as soon as the market picked up. Before long, he had lost his millions and his father's fortune, too. At the time, he didn't even realize the horror of frittering away the money his father had worked a lifetime to save. "I remember my dad came to me and asked me how bad it was," Potekin says. "I told him, 'Dad, it's bad.' Then he starts with figures. 'Do I have $200,000 left?' 'No.' 'Okay, do I have $100,000 left?' 'No.' 'Do we have anything left?' And I said, 'Dad, there's nothing.' 'Nothing?' 'Nothing.' Amazingly, he wasn't even mad at me. All he said was, 'We'll figure out something.' But for me, telling him that his money was gone was one of the hardest things I had to do."

Potekin's fall from his lofty perch was quick and complete. He sold his mansion, his cars, his real estate holdings—even his new furniture. He stayed in the condo on Sheridan Road—on a $50 futon, the only thing in the place—but he stopped paying the mortgage. "It takes a while for them to kick you out," he says. "I was buying time." But soon he was evicted and forced to call a friend. For the next 10 excruciating months, he slept on his friend's small sofa, his head and feet hanging over the sides. "I used to stare at the walls for hours and wonder, 'How the hell did all this happen?' I did my best to cover it up, but deep down I was scared to death."

At one point Potekin found himself with only a single quarter in his pocket. Nothing in the bank, no prospects on the horizon—just 25 cents to his name. "Have you ever walked around with only 25 cents?" he asks. "A lot of crazy fears come into your head when all you own is a quarter. What if I have to make a phone call? What if for some reason I have to get on the bus? What if I need a dollar for something? That was a crazy, crazy way to live." At first, Potekin was in denial about what had happened, but slowly the reality of his dire situation took hold. And as it did, he felt his confidence ebb away. "The experience made me totally insecure. I didn't even have opinions. I've always been an opinionated guy, but I would meet some friends and they would talk about the Cubs and I wouldn't say a word. Because everybody knows what my opinion is worth—nothing! After a while I couldn't even look people in the eye." For 2 long years, Potekin didn't buy himself a single thing. "Are you kidding? I wouldn't even take an aspirin if I had a headache! I would look in the mirror and say, 'You know what? You deserve this headache.' I was punishing myself."

Worst of all, Potekin felt like he had failed his father. "The weight he carried was not for himself, because he could always scratch it out," says his friend Bob Sawyer. "The weight he carried was for his father. He knew he had this image in his father's eyes, and he somehow had to find a way to live up to that image again." But sitting in his friend's apartment and staring at the walls, Potekin could not see a way out of his awful predicament. "I can see why people jump off buildings, that's how weird it gets in your mind," he says. "I even thought about giving up. You know, go to Africa and get some job for $50 a week and just drop out of society. Part of me really wanted to give up."

Then Potekin found himself in that Bagel Nosh on Rush

Street, sharing a plain bagel and a coffee with his dad. "I showed up with like 30 cents in my pocket, hoping that my father had enough to buy us breakfast," he says. "And my father showed up with some coins in his pocket, hoping I had money. Between us we came up with 80 cents." Seeing his father break down in tears, says Potekin, "was the very rock bottom moment for me. I mean, I was befuddled to see him cry. And that's when I said, 'Dad, that's it, we're going to make a comeback. Two years of this nonsense is enough. This part of our life is over as of now.'"

It wasn't just empty talk—Potekin meant it with every fiber of his being. Not even the ordeal of losing his fortune, the humiliation of sleeping on a friend's sofa—the shocking realization that he wasn't as smart as he thought—could wipe out Potekin's belief that he was somehow destined for greatness. "Even when I wanted to give up, there was a part of me that said, 'Barry, you know you can't give up, that's not you.' Deep down, I never, ever gave up hope." Bob Sawyer remembers that, even when things looked bleakest for his friend, Potekin never wallowed in self-pity. "I saw him bottom out, to the point where he had no income, no resources, no investments, no savings," says Sawyer. "He lost everything he had. But even then he didn't lose confidence in himself. No matter how low he got, it just meant that his ship had yet to come in."

Potekin left the Bagel Nosh and returned to his friend's apartment. He sat at the kitchen table and made a list of all the things he thought he could do to change his situation. At the top of the list were two words: fast food. Potekin had a brother, Fred, who managed a restaurant and who would feed him for free three times a week during his darkest days, but beyond that he had no contacts or experience in the restaurant industry. But he remembered how a friend had told him that fast food was the quickest way to get rich with the least amount of money invested up front. Never mind that it wasn't true: at the time it was all that Barry Potekin needed to hear. He decided then and there, at his friend's kitchen table, that he was going to open his own upscale hot dog stand. "Remember, this is Chicago, the No. 1 hot dog town in the country," he says. "There were 3500 hot dogs stands in the city. But my thinking was, no one ever thought of fast food as being upscale. So I decided that I would have to serve the best, freshest hot dogs in town." He ran the idea past his pal Bob Sawyer, not so much for his advice as to let him know that he had finally turned a corner. "Had he asked me for advice, I would have told him what I really thought," says Sawyer. "That it was about the dumbest idea I ever heard. Of all the things in the world, a hot dog stand? I just couldn't see it. But I certainly didn't say anything to discourage Barry. He was all excited again, and that was great to see."

Indeed, Potekin felt the old juices flowing, felt like he could be on top again. "Fear is a great motivator," he says. "But more than that, I had this burning desire to get my money back. I wasn't bitter or anything, I was just determined as hell to make back all the money I lost." But first he had to raise enough money to get his upscale hot dog stand off the drawing board. Potekin went to a few old friends and pitched them on his new idea. He managed to raise $25,000—more than enough, he thought, to open his restaurant. He rented a store in an up-and-coming area called River North, and got to work. But the money ran out about halfway through. Amazingly, he managed to persuade yet another friend to bankroll his hot dog stand. "Put Barry in a sales and marketing position where he believes in what he is selling," says Sawyer, "and the man has no equal."

Potekin's new investor helped him finish the restaurant—almost. A few days before his scheduled opening, Potekin had already reached his spending limit and was still some $15,000 short. "Well, the air conditioning cost about $15,000, and we were opening in January. Who needs air conditioning in January? If we're still open in July, I'll get air conditioning then." Of course, the decision meant that Potekin's restaurant had no heat, either. But at least it would be in business. One day before the grand opening, Potekin had a final hurdle to surmount. "I had exactly $9 in my checking account, which meant that I didn't have enough to pay for food," he recalls. "Somehow I had to come up with that last $150." What Potekin did was make a list of 15 people who had refused to lend him money in the past. Then he rang 15 doorbells and asked to borrow $10 from each friend. "I figured that most people wouldn't mind lending me 10 bucks. And all 15 people did, though some of them didn't do it all that nicely."

On January 14, 1985, Potekin's restaurant—a 1000-square-foot, 35-seat corner store he called Gold Coast Dogs—finally opened its doors. His father and mother were behind the counter, since Potekin couldn't afford to pay employees. He made about $800, enough to open for business on day 2. That second day, Potekin's butcher showed up with a bill for $80. "He comes in and of course I can't pay him, so I tell him, 'I'll be right with you,'" says Potekin. "I throw four or five hamburgers on the grill, and when I sell them I go out and give the butcher $10 and I tell him, 'Hold on another second, I'll be right back.' I throw some more burgers and franks on, I bring out another $10. He's like, 'What the heck is going on?' But I paid him his $80 in 20 minutes."

Potekin did whatever he could to drum up business. He'd walk the streets and corral perfect strangers, and usher them into

Gold Coast Dogs to try his food for free. "There are 35,000 hot dogs stands, and the people in all of them stand around the register and wait for customers to come in. That's no way to run a business. I would walk up and down the streets, talking to strangers all day long. 'Hi, my name is Barry and I just opened a restaurant around the corner. Come on in, lunch is on me.' They thought I was nuts! But I really believed in my heart that my food was better, and so I told them 'If you like the food, do me a favor and tell your friends.' Plus, I couldn't afford advertising, so what else was I going to do?" Potekin would also take five cab rides every day, convincing cabbies to steer their fares to his upscale fast food joint. "There are a million cabbies in Chicago," he points out. "So every day I would take five cab rides to nowhere. I'd hop in, make up an address downtown, and spend the whole time bending the cabbie's ear. And when I got downtown, I'd pay my fare and give the cabby a $5 certificate to eat at Gold Coast. And then I'd hop another cab and start all over again." Bit by bit—cabby by cabby—Potekin was developing a steady clientele.

Then something really remarkable happened. Six months after he opened, the *Chicago Sun Times* wrote that Gold Coast had the very best hot dog in Chicago. Not long after that, the *Chicago Tribune* picked his hamburger as the best in town. "Who would have dreamed that would happen?" Potekin says. "After that, the place is rocking, absolutely jumping! The people are lining up down the street!" Barry Potekin's ship had come in once again.

●●●

Today, there are 15 Gold Coast Dogs restaurants. Potekin and a partner, a business wizard named Paul Michaels, began franchising the operation, and now 11 of the 15 Gold Coasts are franchised, with more to come. Potekin's yearly revenues are in the millions and growing every year. His freshly prepared franks, hamburgers, and grilled swordfish sandwiches—introduced precisely when newly dubbed "yuppies" were seizing on any upscale experience—have been celebrated in *Fortune, USA Today, People, The Wall Street Journal* and the *Today Show*, and Potekin himself has won several entrepreneurial awards. Even David Letterman dubbed Potekin's franks "the best hot dogs in the country." On top of all that, Gold Coast Dogs got the chance to cater Hillary Clinton's 50th birthday party in Chicago. "I went up to President Clinton and shook his hand and made a little small talk," says Potekin. "And I'm standing there, thinking, 'Can you believe this, I'm chatting up the President? Me, the guy who was sleeping on a sofa only a few years back?' "

That humility is one big difference between the Barry Potekin of today and the fellow who threw away imperfect shirts and dirty kitchenware. Which is not to say that Potekin is any less driven. "I have the same burning desire to succeed that I had 20 years ago," he says. "No matter what I'm doing—eating dinner, watching a movie, whatever—in the back of my mind I'm thinking about my business. I'm thinking about how to separate myself from the herd. To be successful you have to be a diamond in a barrel of marbles. And that was my thinking even when times were tough." Even then, Potekin somehow summoned the confidence to open a hot dog stand in Chicago—sort of like opening a pasta place in Rome. "A friend of mine was a Ranger in the Army, and he told me that the first rule of war is audacity! Don't train to survive, train to win! Some countries teach their soldiers how to survive in combat, and those countries always end up losing wars. You have to be audacious to succeed!"

Potekin's journey through the forest of loss only strengthened his resolve to be a winner. That, perhaps, was the greatest lesson he learned. "Everyone has that winning flame burning inside of them," he says. "You just have to work very hard to keep that flame alive. You have to realize that very few things are the end of the world. Go out there and give it your best shot, and if it doesn't work out, hey, it's not the end of the world. Believe me, I know."

For Barry Potekin, the coffee cup is always half full.

TIPS FOR TOUGH TIMES

The Barry Potekin Story

When a man is pushed, tormented, defeated, he has a chance to learn something; he has been put on his wits; on his manhood; he has gained the facts.

Ralph Waldo Emerson

Barry Potekin went from living in a mansion and buying custom-made shirts by the dozen to sleeping on a friend's sofa and not being able to buy a bagel. That sort of journey just has to be edifying. The real tragedy isn't falling from grace, as Potekin did. The real tragedy is not learning from the experience. A mistake remains a mistake if it's repeated; it becomes a stepping stone to success if we learn from it.

And, as often happens, the circumstances of our failures make it possible for us to achieve real success. The things we learn about ourselves in defeat embolden us to reach for goals we never dreamed of reaching. Potekin's early success as a gold and silver trader obscured the fact that he was neither a particularly good businessperson nor a particularly good human being. It was only after he failed spectacularly that he could put the pieces back together in a way that made for a better, richer life. Small wonder that so many people who *crash and burn—Barry Potekin included—say they wouldn't trade the experience of failing for anything in the world.*

1. **Find the Real Reason You Failed**   Before self-renewal can take place, a full accounting of what happened is necessary. It is not helpful to rationalize or otherwise underplay your failures. Take a good, long look in the mirror and face the cold, hard facts. Potekin spent long weeks staring at walls and mumbling to himself, trying to assess exactly what went wrong. He finally realized that he had been done in by own hubris, his immaturity, his lack of foresight and solid business sense—and not by the vagaries of the gold and silver markets. That was the first step in his comeback. *Assess the weaknesses that led to your failure and vow to turn them into strengths.*

2. **Hitting Bottom Means You're On Your Way Up**   It's hard to find any positives in life when you're sleeping on a friend's sofa and too broke to afford a cup of coffee. But as Potekin learned from hitting bottom, "very few things are the end of the world." In fact, hitting bottom can be a cathartic, liberating experience. Potekin was stripped of everything he owned, and so he had nothing to lose when he opened his hot dog business. Because he had no obligations, expectations, or other entanglements, he was free to change gears, choose a new direction,

and just take off. *Failure is not the end of the world, but rather the beginning of a bold, new journey.*

3. **Don't Let Failure Make You Fearful—Be Audacious!** The best thing about Potekin's bold, new journey was that he was undertaking it as a changed and different man. When he was a gold and silver trader, he was cocky, fearless, even arrogant, but ultimately lacking in the maturity to weather difficult times. Potekin's act was all sizzle and no substance. After his failure, he discovered a strength and willpower he never knew he had. As he put it, he emerged from the dark forest a better, wiser man. Thus, he didn't allow failure to make him skittish or tentative—he approached each new challenge with unprecedented audacity. He didn't train to survive, he trained to win. *Failure builds character and unearths hidden strengths; use these new resources to chase your goals with more determination than ever.*

4. RECIPE FOR SUCCESS

The Linda Fisher Story

It's like Victor Mature said in the movie Samson and Delilah: *"Thank you, God, for taking away my sight, so that I may truly see."*

Linda Fisher

She felt ashamed to walk down the streets of her town. Hundreds and hundreds of times before Linda Fisher had walked the lovely streets of Westminster, a pleasant little city in northern Maryland. Behind her she always pulled her rusted red Radio Flyer wagon, stacked to capacity with dozens of piping hot muffins, baked only hours before in her tiny kitchen.

The muffins—banana nut, peach cobbler, white chocolate, and other mouth-watering flavors—were fashioned from her mother Catherine's legendary pancake batter recipe, and so they were richer, sweeter, more delicious than any muffins anyone in town had ever tasted. Every morning, Linda Fisher would make her regular rounds, visiting friends at the flower shop, the radio station, the savings bank, the dry cleaners, even the local government office. And every day her friends would happily dole out $1.25 for one of Fisher's magical 6-ounce muffins. Her visits became part of their daily routine, part of the precious fabric of communal life in friendly Westminster. Linda Fisher became a popular fixture—the Muffin Lady, everyone called her—and more importantly she earned enough money to raise her young son Olivier.

But then, one cold January morning in 1997, three county health officials stopped Fisher in an alley. They told her that she had to stop selling muffins she baked in her kitchen, that she was violating strict food preparation laws. They told her she faced a fine of up to $1000 a day and even 90 days in the county jail. After that day, Fisher put her wagon away and stopped baking altogether. Even worse, she stopped visiting her friends, stopped strolling the streets of her very own town. "I felt ashamed," she explains. "I was just so embarrassed by the whole situation. I had been doing business with all of these people, passing myself off as a legitimate businessperson, and then this happened and word got out that I was not legitimate. I felt like I had let my friends down, and so I felt ashamed to walk the streets. I didn't know how they would react to seeing me. I traveled around incognito, hiding my face as much as I could."

Things got so bad that Fisher even thought about skipping town altogether. "That's how much of a failure I felt like," she says. "Honestly, I was really ready to give up. I felt scared and ashamed and just ready to pack up and go. I didn't know how all these people would react to me."

Soon, Linda Fisher would find out what the people of Westminster thought of her. And it wasn't what she expected at all.

●●●

Baking muffins was in Fisher's blood, as much an inheritance from her mother as her beaming smile and happy eyes. Growing up in Washington, DC, young Linda learned that life revolved around the kitchen, where her mother, Catherine, whipped up lavish meals for the family. "What I remember most of all was her Saturday morning meal—pancakes," says Fisher. "They were light and fluffy, the most delicious things you can imagine. And add a little maple syrup...*mmm, mmm.*" Bit by bit, Fisher learned the tricks of the trade from her mom—how to tell when a dish was ready by smell and not by timer, how to add ingredients by feel and not by measuring cup. Recipes were revealed in small doses, secrets shared only over time. "I was 11 when I started helping out in the kitchen," says Fisher, whose first solo dish was a batch of cornbread. "By the time I was 15 I was an old hand, and my mother cut me loose to make whatever I wanted."

At 17, she received the highest compliment her mother could bestow—a request to make the cornbread for the Thanksgiving turkey stuffing. "That was quite a responsibility," says Fisher. "I felt really proud when I pulled it off." It was, she says, the day she arrived as a baker.

After that, she was pressed into service as often as 5 days a week, while her activist parents spent long evenings attending meetings and social events. "They were really into improving the environment for their children," says Fisher. "But it meant that they often didn't get home until 10 or 11. Well, we all had to eat, so somebody had to prepare the food. And because I was the eldest sister, I was supposed to get the meals ready."

It was excellent training and would serve her well in years to come. But early on, Fisher had no plans to enter the food industry. "No, no, no, my family was about education," she says. "Any kind of job that even hinted of slavery, they were dead set against. They never wanted me to go into baking professionally." When she turned 18, Fisher married her high school sweetheart, and the two moved into their own apartment in Washington, DC. Through her husband, Fisher met the second most pivotal woman in her life—his grandmother Veronica. "She was just this incredible, unbelievable person," says Fisher. "Years back, she had been the housekeeper for J. W. Marriott, and she was just this amazing professional in the kitchen. This woman birthed four children, and each of them birthed at least four children, so she was used to cooking meals for a lot of people. And I really learned a lot from her, not only about cooking but about life."

She and her husband had two children before they went their separate ways. "We were young and we just weren't ready for marriage," she says. "I was still living in a fantasy world, and he was all too real. And so those two worlds would clash every day." Her ex-husband took care of the kids, while Fisher found a good, secure job with Blue Cross & Blue Shield. But 5 years later she had a major disagreement with a supervisor, and left the job in a huff. "I was really out there on a high wire after that," she says. "It was 2 weeks before Christmas, and suddenly I was in dire straits. I didn't even have enough money to buy my children Christmas presents." Fisher felt lost, desperate, unsure of what to do. "I literally cried out to God to help me," she recalls. "And He did. That day, 2 weeks before Christmas, in my apartment in Washington, DC, I heard the voice of God."

His message was to the point: "He said, 'I want you to bake,'" Fisher recalls. "I mean, it was so simple, I couldn't believe it. Here was the answer, just like that! Honestly, I hadn't ever dreamed I would bake for a living before that day."

Fisher heeded her spiritual revelation and baked a bunch of carrot cakes in the days before Christmas. She sold them to her former coworkers at Blue Cross, and made a quick $300, which she used to buy clothes for her children. "These were people who already knew about my baking, and so when I called them they were like, 'Yeah, Linda, come on down!' And it was whatever I felt like baking—brownies, cookies, pound cake, you name it. Soon people started placing orders."

Through a friend she got a client at the State Department in Washington, DC. "One day I brought over all my stuff and set it out in this room for all the people to pick up," she recalls. "Well, as the room got crowded with everyone picking up their orders, this one gentleman came up to me and sort of just stood there beside me." Then the man said something that forever changed Fisher's life. "He said, 'Have you ever thought of going commercial?' And it was like a light bulb going off."

●●●

Just like that, Linda Fisher got into wholesale baking. By then, she had married for a second time, another union that, sadly, would not last. "I met my second husband on a blind date on Halloween," she says. "I like to say that first I got the treat, then I got the trick." Fisher's business, though, was going more smoothly. She started selling cakes to a West African restaurant in the chic Adams Morgan section of Washington, DC, churning them out one at a time in her small oven. "Then this prominent food critic wrote a great review of the restaurant, and overnight the owner increased his order from five to 20 cakes a week. A month later the critic panned the restaurant, and he dropped me altogether. That's the way it goes, I guess."

It was a tough but important lesson for Fisher to learn. Jobs and clients would come and go, but the skills she had—her baking expertise—would never go away. Her confidence was soaring, her self-esteem at an all-time high. She took her carrot cake over to a deli in a Georgetown mall, and followed that by snagging gigs in several upscale restaurants in the Washington, DC, area. "That's when the business really got going," she says. "I was in the right restaurants, I was meeting the right people—they were even offering me the use of their kitchens and not even charging me! My baking business was taking off." Shortly after this surge in demand, Fisher—involved with but not married to a third man—gave birth to her third child, a son they named Olivier.

Unfortunately, the delivery did not go well. "I got really sick, so sick I couldn't even walk," says Fisher. "My doctors told me I had to choose between my baby and my business." And so Fisher gave up baking, staying home to take care of her child and nurse herself to better health. What she didn't realize was how attached to baking she had become, how much a part of her spiritual health making cakes and muffins was. "I discovered that I really needed to work," she says. "Not so much for the money, but for my mental stability. I had come this far, and I had this thing that was really successful for me. And I really didn't want to give that up." Six weeks later, she was back in the kitchen, baking again.

The only problem—in those 6 weeks she had lost all of her 22 accounts.

●●●

It might have been a devastating setback, but by then Fisher knew a thing or two about adversity. She also had a pretty good handle on the finer points of salesmanship. "What I learned is that you have to sell yourself before you sell your product. Once they fall in love with you, they will deal with whatever you offer them."

Fisher called up her friends in the fancy restaurants, and quickly re-signed 10 of her most lucrative accounts.

Craving steadier work, Fisher took a baking job at Catholic University, her first official union job. She got married for a third time, and followed her husband to his jobs in New Jersey, and then Rochester, New York. Finally, she persuaded him to move the family to Westminster, Maryland, as close as his job would send him to the South that Fisher loved so much. Once again, her marriage fell apart, but at least she had a solid job as an assistant manager at a senior citizen's residential facility. "I thought I would have that job a long, long time," she says. "But then they had some budget problems, and I was out on the street again." Just like that she was back at square one—and wouldn't you know it, it was right before Christmas again.

It had been nearly 20 years since her first spiritual revelation, and suddenly it was time for another. "I was sitting in my apartment, wondering what to do, when it sort of dawned on me that, 'You're a baker, so make the most of it!' It was the same message He had sent me all those years earlier. I had flour in the house, I had a sugar in the house, so what was I waiting for? I was like, 'Okay, let's do this again.'"

Her life had often been as messy as a six-course meal prepared in a studio kitchen. And so when tough times came around, Fisher had learned to keep her cool and simply roll with the punches. One day, a freak storm dumped 16 inches of snow on Westminster. Most people saw it as a hardship, a bad break, a reason to complain. But Fisher saw it as something far more wondrous—an opportunity. "Remember, I had spent some time in Rochester in upstate New York," she says. "So 16 inches of snow was nothing to me. But I knew these people in Westminster would be freaking out and staying indoors, and that gave me a chance to get to them."

Fisher baked six blueberry muffins in her kitchen, packed them tightly in a basket, and made her way through the snow to the local radio station a few blocks from her house. She walked in, asked if she could leave the basket, and propped an empty envelope next to her fresh batch of muffins. "They were 50 cents each, and it was all on the honor system," she says. "I knew I couldn't just walk in there and expect them to buy my muffins. I had to do it on consignment." A little while later she came back and took a look inside the envelope. It held $3 in change—and all six muffins were gone. "The receptionist told me I could bring muffins again, but there was a stipulation—I had to do it every day. And just like that I was on my way."

More snow hit Westminster, and Fisher decided to schlep some muffins over to the local school. Soon people started noticing Fisher walking the mile between the school and the station, her basket of steaming muffins on her shoulder. "They would come up to me and ask me where I was going, and then they would ask, 'Can I buy a muffin right now?' " she says. "Word of mouth started spreading like wildfire." Fisher picked up several clients along her route, and then got lucky when Westminster's district attorney visited the radio station and got a taste of her blueberry muffins. "He got a hold of me and asked me if I could do for his office what I was doing for the radio station. Only he needed double the number of muffins. Well, I would walk over to his office on the third floor, and I would pass all these government agencies on the way. And the aroma of these muffins would waft all over, and people would come out to see what was going on. And that's how my muffins really caught on—it was almost impossible for them *not* to catch on." Before she knew it, Fisher was delivering her muffins to 27 offices.

The secret, of course, was that she made her muffins with pancake batter, something she started doing years earlier. "It was my mother's original recipe for pancakes, but she never used it for muffins," Fisher explains. "I got the idea when one of my clients asked me for a special type of muffin. He described it in detail and asked me if I could do it, and of course I said yes right away even though I had no idea how it could be done. But by then it was ingrained in me that I was a baker by trade, and I felt pretty confident in the kitchen." Fisher went home, fooled around with a few recipes, and suddenly decided to try her mother's pancake batter. "It must have been a divine inspiration, because it worked right away," she says. "I had to get the measurements down, but it was pretty successful from the start. Of course, the man loved his muffin and became a loyal customer."

Fisher's muffins were so popular in Westminster, she couldn't keep up with demand. "At one point I was carrying six dozen items everyday! That's 72 muffins on my shoulders! I had to max out at that because I knew I couldn't carry any more." One of her clients noticed Fisher's burden and suggested she get some kind of transportation. But, unfortunately, Fisher did not drive. "So this woman told me she would get me some wheels, and the next day she gave me this red Radio Flyer wagon she had in her garage. It was rusted and a little banged up, but it was pretty solid. And it did the job."

Business was booming for the newly christened Muffin Lady of Westminster. And yet it was far from an easy time for Fisher. For one thing, she had to wake up at midnight to bake her muffins, and would steal a little extra sleep after they were all delivered by mid-morning. And while the money she made on her route helped her and her young son survive, it wasn't always enough for her to make ends meet. Eventually, she couldn't afford her house in the suburbs, and had to give it up. Social services set her up in a government-subsidized townhouse, but Fisher was determined to keep her family off welfare. "Yeah, I lost my house, but I wasn't going to also end up on welfare," she says. "I had a trade and I wanted to work! I didn't want to get caught up in the system. I didn't want it for me, and I sure didn't want it for Olivier. I was very determined to make my business work."

And work it did, quite wonderfully, much to the delight of Fisher's more-than-satisfied customers. "I mean, everybody wanted her muffins, they were so good," says Ginger Hornberger of the Flower Box, one of the stops along Fisher's route. "She got so many orders that she couldn't keep up with them, even with the wagon. Everybody looked forward to her coming and to buying her muffins. She had a great product, and as a person she had a wonderful spirit, too." It seemed like a sweet, idyllic slice of small-town life, a tribute to Westminster's values and togetherness. Thanks to her own skills and ingenuity—and to the enthusiastic support of her friends in town—Linda Fisher was a true American success story. "I had my townhouse, I had my business, everything was okay," Fisher says. "It finally looked like I was going to be okay for a while."

● ● ●

Then, on January 8, 1997, Fisher was walking her route as usual, and found herself in an alley along James Street. Suddenly a car was circling her, getting closer until it pulled up alongside her. "Two women and a man in suits got out and came up to me,"

Fisher recalls. "One of the women said excuse me and asked me to stop. But I had my walkman on and I didn't pay any attention. I was in Linda's world."

The woman finally blocked Fisher's path, and introduced herself as an official of the Carroll County Health Department. "She said, 'It is our understanding that you are baking your muffins out of your kitchen. As of today you are ordered to cease and desist.' " The problem was that Fisher's kitchen was not equipped with an open drain, which violated certain health department codes. The penalty for selling her muffins, should Fisher decide to continue, would be a $1000 daily fine and as much as 90 days in jail. "I just threw my hands up and said, 'Girl, the game is up,' " says Fisher. "The way they approached me was very intimidating, and they spooked me pretty good."

The woman who had endured so many setbacks finally felt defeated. "I went home, curled up in a fetal position, and got really depressed," Fisher says. "I mean, they were killing me economically, and there was nothing I could do." Worst of all for Fisher was that news of the incident spread so quickly through Westminster. "It's a small town and of course everybody knew what happened. And that just made me feel completely ashamed."

She had always traveled everywhere with a mile-wide smile on her face. But now Fisher hung her head when she dared venture into town, afraid that she would be recognized and asked about what happened. "I just felt like I wanted to be left alone. I didn't want to face anyone, didn't want to know how they'd react. I felt like a total failure, and I was ready to pack it in."

Slinking away in shame, leaving her friends behind, giving up the thing she did the best of all—it would have been a sad and miserable ending to Fisher's saga. But then something amazing happened in the sleepy hamlet of Westminster. The story of Fisher's "bust" by the health department ran in the local paper, and the next day Fisher got a call from a friend at social services. "She said, 'Linda, you won't believe this, but the fire department is offering you the use of their kitchen for free!' " Fisher recalls. "And she was right, I couldn't believe it. I was touched, I hadn't expected that. I was overwhelmed."

The Carroll County Health Department checked out the spacious galley kitchen at Westminster's volunteer fire department, and gave the okay for Fisher to bake her muffins there. An anonymous donation of $60 helped Fisher get the license she needed to resume her business. Three weeks after she had been sidelined, Fisher showed up at the fire department at 2:00 a.m. and got right back to work. She whipped up several dozen muffins, loaded up her trusty Radio Flyer, and got ready to walk her route again.

But facing her friends again proved difficult. "That first day back, I was scared to death," says Fisher. "After all this hoopla I was afraid of how people would react to me. I almost couldn't bring myself to get back out there again." The ordeal had dented Fisher's confidence, damaged the self-esteem she had built over years as a professional baker. It was the weight of failure that she felt, the shame of letting people down. Such is the stigma of defeat that it left Fisher wondering if her friends would be there for her. "Would it be the same? Would they look at me differently? I was really scared that maybe I had lost them as friends."

It wouldn't take long for her to find out.

• • •

Fisher took a deep breath, tightened the bungee cords on her wagon, and set out on her route once again. Before long, clients were rushing out of their homes to greet her, hugging her and kissing her and telling her how happy they were that she was back. "It was just about the most emotional day of my life," she says. "It was overwhelming. And every stop along the way was the same, with my friends coming out and hugging and kissing me. I mean, they were *elated* to have me back!" Ginger Hornberger of the Flower Box remembers that happy day. "The whole county opened up its arms to her," says Hornberger. "The outpouring of support for her was really something to see. Everybody up and down the main drag was happy to see her, happy to have her back. It was really a wonderful day when she returned."

For every muffin she sold that day, Fisher shed a hundred tears. All the love she had put into baking had come back to her a thousand times over. It took the humiliating failure of being put out of business for Fisher to realize just how her friends felt about her. "The warmth and kindness that I received that day," she says, "was the greatest gift I could ever get."

The story of Fisher's triumphant return soon landed her on "Good Morning America" and in *The Washington Post*. Before long, she signed a book deal, and her wonderful collection of amazing recipes and life lessons—*The Muffin Lady: Muffins, Cupcakes and Quick Breads for the Happy Soul*—still sells nicely on Amazon.com. "She handled adversity really well," says her friend Ginger Hornberger. "She's been at the bottom of the barrel and she somehow worked her way back out. She's a very caring, strong-willed person, the kind of underdog you like to root for." Fisher herself sees what happened to her as part of God's master plan for her. "It's like Victor Mature said in the movie *Samson and Delilah*: 'Thank you, God, for taking away my sight, so that I may truly see.' God took away my sight, my comfort, and that's how I discovered what was what."

These days, Fisher is living in New Orleans, working on a book about the city's invisible poor. Her smart and handsome son Olivier is now 17 and on his way to college, and he will serve as a testament to Fisher's perseverance. "He's doing well and he makes me proud," she says. "It just goes to show you that part of life is paying your dues. You keep yourself focused on the future, you learn from your mistakes, and you move on."

"Really, it's as simple as that."

TIPS FOR TOUGH TIMES

The Linda Fisher Story

The greatest test of courage on earth is to bear defeat without losing heart.

Robert G. Ingersoll

Linda Fisher very nearly gave up when the Carroll County health officials put her out of business. She was a baker down to her bones, and yet they were telling her that she could not bake. Even worse, she was being humiliated in front of all her friends. She felt like a complete failure in their eyes. Defeats don't come much more disheartening than that.

But Fisher didn't give up or move out of town. She got a lucky break, and then she set out on her route again, despite her apprehension about how her friends would treat her. The warm and happy reception she received was a blessing that Fisher might have missed had she slunk out of town. And it was only possible after the heartbreak of her defeat. By then, of course, Fisher was no stranger to enduring hard times. She did not think in terms of failures and successes—she thought more in terms of bumps in the road that had to be traversed. Like the recipes her mother handed down to her, her approach to handling adversity was simple—get past it somehow, then go on.

1. **You Won't Get Everything Right the First Time** Fisher learned this lesson in the kitchen, where messy setbacks are the rule, not the exception. And, in life as well, goals are rarely accomplished right out of the chute. Fisher had to try different jobs and consider different goals before it dawned on her that baking was the thing she was meant to do. And even after that she had to win and lose several clients before she found her greatest success as a baker. What kept her going was her stark and simple goal—make enough money to support her young son and stay off welfare. *Setbacks, mishaps and out-and-out failures are steps that lead you closer to success.*

2. **Accept That Paying Dues Is Part of the Deal** Navigating those steps and bumps will not always be easy. Some appear impossibly steep, and many times it takes sacrifice and hardship to surmount them. But as Fisher learned in the kitchen, nothing great can be created without a little elbow grease. No one should expect to rise to his or her desired heights without a few kicks in the shins from fate; in fact, they should feel cheated if their path to the top is unencumbered. *The battles and sacrifices along the way are what enrich you as a person and make your ultimate success the sweetest dish in the world.*

3. **Do What You Do with Love, and You'll Be Rewarded** Flour and sugar were not the most important ingredients in Linda Fisher's muffins—love was. Without it, she would

have been just another baker, and not the beloved Muffin Lady embraced by an entire town. The lesson here is that success and failure are incidental considerations—the one thing that you can control is how you do your work. True greatness is the result of extraordinary effort coupled with a genuine love for the task. Fisher never made a muffin that wasn't baked with pride and passion—with the love that her mother and her grandmother passed on to her. That is why, when she hit tough times, her friends were there to pick her up—to return the love they always received from her. *No matter how rough the going gets, keep doing what you do with dignity and pride—for that is a reward in itself.*

5 BACK FROM THE BRINK

The Ben Beltzer Story

We all need people to believe in us, so that we can believe in ourselves.

Ben Beltzer

Just like Jimmy Stewart in *It's a Wonderful Life*, Ben Beltzer figured he was worth more dead than alive. So much was going wrong in his life, so many things were falling apart. He used to be a rich and confident businessman, living in a big house and driving a big car, and he never thought for a moment that this could happen to him. But here he was, 40 years old and the father of four young children, and he had no job, no money, no hope. Worst of all, he had been forced to go on welfare, something no Beltzer had ever done before. "I decided that the best thing for me to do, since I still had a life insurance policy, was to commit suicide," Beltzer recalls. "That way at least my family would have resources." So he took his gun, one of the few things he hadn't sold, and he found a quiet spot behind a church not far from where he lived. Then he sat on a log and gripped the pistol and got ready to end it all.

But something happened as he sat on the log that changed his life profoundly. In turn, Beltzer has had a profound effect on the lives of hundreds and hundreds of people. Today, Beltzer runs the Interfaith Housing Coalition in Dallas, Texas. The coalition is a unique, not-for-profit program that helps homeless families get on their feet by giving them temporary housing, a range of training, and, most importantly, a bombardment of support. The program is so successful that it has won a slew of awards and been copied in several states, becoming a model of "transitional housing," a concept that may replace welfare in the new millenium. The reason it works, plain and simple, is because of Ben Beltzer—and because of what he learned from standing in welfare lines. "What happened to me is a miracle," he says, "a miracle born of community."

He didn't always believe in miracles, at least not until one fateful night when he was 19 years old. Never very religious as a youngster growing up in Kirksville, Missouri, Beltzer was an aimless teenager when he decided to enlist in the Navy. Out partying with a few fellow sailors one weekend, Beltzer got himself good and drunk. "I ran back to the car to get some more booze, and I caught my reflection in the car's side window," he remembers. "And for some reason it scared the heck out of me. I didn't like what I saw." Beltzer dropped the booze and ran away, ran right to the First Baptist Church of Port Isabel, Texas. "I woke up this preacher and said, 'I was drunk and now I'm sober and I need some help,' " says Beltzer. "He took me in, fed me breakfast, and invited me to attend the Church. And that was the beginning of a real spiritual experience for me."

Beltzer became an ordained minister, married Patsy, a fellow churchgoer, and spent the next 10 years as a pastor in four different cities. Along the way, he got a degree in business administration, and eventually became the national credit manager for a major corporation. As part of a little consulting business he ran on the side, Beltzer traveled to Kansas City to evaluate a struggling tire company. "It was about a quarter million in the red, and I advised the owner to go bankrupt, close it down, and get out," says Beltzer. "And for some reason, he just looked at me and asked me if I wanted to take the company over." Beltzer's reaction? "Absolutely not! I had run all the figures, and they didn't look good."

Still, Beltzer liked the owner, who was a solid, Christian man. And something inside him was intrigued by the challenge of turning a company around. "Long story short, I took a leave of absence from my job and took the company over," he says. "To this day I don't know why I did it. In retrospect it was providence, considering all the changes wrought by that one decision." Beltzer's deal with the owner was that he would do his best to get the company out of the red, and that if he succeeded 85 percent of the stock would be his. For a man with a wife, four kids, and a steady full-time job, it was quite a gamble to take.

But Beltzer did what he set out to do—he turned the company around. He sold off one division, streamlined operations, and soon put the balance sheet firmly in the black. Beltzer quit his full-time job, and within 2½ years the company became one of only 34 national distributors of Dunlop Tires. Profits rolled in, and Beltzer built a sprawling, five-bedroom home in an affluent section of Liberty, Missouri. Business was so good that he decided it was the perfect time to sell the company and clean up on his stock deal.

There was, however, one little problem. "The agreement between me and the previous owner was a verbal agreement," says Beltzer. "I never had a problem with that because that's the way my father always handled things. He would shake a man's hand

and that was as good as gold." Beltzer went ahead with the sale, but in the end all the money went to the original owner. The man who turned the company around got nothing. Incredibly, Beltzer was not bitter or resentful about this turn of events. "It was my error, and I surely learned my lesson," he says. "I was not mad at the owner and I cannot blame him for what he did. Sure, I was frustrated, but the truth is I wasn't all that worried. I had plenty of savings, and I figured I would go out and get a job the next day. It just didn't seem like the end of the world at all."

•••

Still, there he was, 40 years old with four young kids, and out of work for the first time ever. Early on, he did not change his lavish lifestyle much; Beltzer retained his personal secretary, who would dutifully type up his résumé and send it out to dozens of companies. His savings were steadily dwindling, sure, but it was only a matter of time, he thought, before someone snapped him up. A few days passed, and then a few weeks, and before he knew it 5 months had gone by. "That's when I realized, 'Hey, wait a minute, nobody seems all that interested in me getting a job.' "

First, Beltzer let his personal secretary go. Then he cut back on other expenses. Soon he had to sell all the new furniture he bought for his new house. Before he knew it, all of his savings were gone, and something like depression was starting to set in. Bit by bit, his confidence and self-esteem was eroding. The light at the end of the tunnel was growing dimmer and dimmer. No longer was he losing sleep about finding work; now he was sweating out where the next hot meal would come from. Most mornings, Beltzer couldn't even find the strength to get out of bed.

That's when he learned about the importance of community. Five men from his church, five good friends, took it upon themselves to help this lost soul find his way. They didn't do it by giving him money or guiding him in any one direction; they simply made sure that he never gave up hope. "What they did was hold me accountable for my own dreams," says Beltzer. "They took turns calling me in the morning, making sure I got up and got dressed and went out and looked for a job. They never imposed their own ideas on me, they just made sure I didn't give up on my own goals and dreams." When Beltzer finally ran out of savings, it was the five men who made sure he signed up for unemployment. Left to his own, he wouldn't have done it, proud man that he was. In fact, the first time he went to the government office, he saw how full the parking lot was and turned his car around. One of the five men called him that night and asked him how it went. After some firm encouragement, Beltzer drove back to the office the next day. This time he got as far as the front door, where he peered into the window at the long lines inside and did a quick about-face. Once again, the five men made sure Beltzer took a third trip. This time he made it all the way in and signed up for his benefits.

The men didn't scold Beltzer or drag him kicking and screaming to the office. They just made sure that he went on his own, that he did not feel too sorry for himself. Not long after signing up for unemployment, Beltzer had to make the painful decision to sign up for welfare as well. "Going to the welfare office was the most humiliating thing I have ever experienced in my life," he says. "I never thought a Beltzer would have to do that. Never in a million years did I think that." Despite the unyielding support of his five friends, Beltzer sank deeper and deeper into despair. Finally, he lost the home that he had built, and moved his family into a small one-bedroom apartment he could barely afford. "I guess the rock bottom moment was the day I lost my house," he recalls. "That's when I decided to commit suicide, thinking that my family would do better without me."

The day after he made that decision, Beltzer left his apartment early without telling his wife where he was going. Sure enough, one of the five men called and asked about Ben. Patsy, his wife, said she didn't know where he was, but that she was very worried. Beltzer went to a local youth center, and took a seat on a log out back, just behind a chapel. It was a quiet, peaceful, secluded spot, and Beltzer sat there for the longest time, thinking about what he was about to do, about how things had so quickly come to this. He held the loaded gun in his pocket, and tried to make his final peace with the Lord. It will be better this way, he told himself. This is what you have to do. "It was," says Beltzer, "the bottom of the abyss."

He didn't hear his friend come up behind him; he only felt it when the friend put his arm around his shoulder. "I still don't know how he knew where I was," says Beltzer. "To this day, I still don't know." The friend sat beside him on the log and talked to him for the longest time. Together they got up, walked around, and went back home. These were Beltzer's first, tentative steps up from the bottom, toward the light.

The five friends kept calling, kept trying to lift his spirits. When Christmas rolled around, and Beltzer didn't have money to buy his children gifts, some neighbors made sure that each of the four received at least one present. When his eldest daughter needed a new dress to wear to the prom, a woman from the church brought over a beautiful satin gown for the girl to wear. "They did these things in a way that never made me feel like I was accepting charity," says Beltzer. "What I felt like I was experiencing was the love of a neighbor. It was a powerful, powerful experience for me, and it was how I rebuilt my self-esteem."

Slowly but surely, Beltzer was getting back on his feet. He went to a friend who owned a gas station and asked him for a job. The only thing available was a position pumping gas for $4.75 an hour. His boss would be a 20- year-old who used to work for him at the tire company. Beltzer took it anyway. Standing out in the cold weather, pumping gas into cars that belonged to wealthy former business associates, Beltzer often looked to the heavens and asked, "God, what is the matter with you? What am I doing out here pumping gas?"

The moments of self-pity passed, and Beltzer soon devised a plan. He heard about a service station that was up for sale, and he took the idea of him buying it to his five loyal friends. The morning the deal was set to close, one of the five showed up at Beltzer's apartment with a check for $25,000. The light was growing brighter and brighter; Beltzer was back in business again.

He worked hard, made the service station profitable, and paid off all his debts. Then he moved his family into a bigger, better house. Now he just had to make some sense of all that he had gone through. He came to the conclusion that there was a lesson in all his suffering. "Through my journey I came to see poor people in a different light," he says. "Before, when someone mentioned the poor to me, I threw some money at them. But now that I had stood in welfare lines with them, I saw that the pains of hunger they felt, the low self-esteem they felt, the total and complete humiliation they endured, were no different than what I had experienced myself." Beltzer brainstormed with some volunteers from his church and came up with the concept of transitional housing. Families going through hard times would stay in homes—not shelters—for 3 or 4 months, learn basic living skills, get help looking for jobs, and receive the constant encouragement of an army of volunteers. The concept was based on the crucial support that Beltzer received from his five friends. "I would not have been strong enough to survive had it not been for my community," he says. "There were things inside of me that their support brought out. What I learned was that no man is an island; we all need people around us every day. We all need people to believe in us, so that we can believe in ourselves."

•••

Thus, the Interfaith Housing Coalition was born. In 1985 Beltzer moved the operation to Dallas, where he still lives with his wife, Patsy. Today, the Coalition has nine paid full-time staffers, some 200 volunteers, and two apartment complexes totaling roughly 31 units. Its operating budget is $750,000 (raised through donations and not a single government cent) and helps about 100 families every year. Some people refer to Beltzer's methods as tough love, but he prefers to say he is holding people accountable for their own dreams. Families who come through the program are expected to complete educational training, find employment, secure their own apartments, and save $1200—all in the space of 90 to 120 days. Far from discovering that poor people need a lot of time to get their acts together, Beltzer found out that most of them were eager to change their lives. All they needed was a little help in finding a way out. "They were extended the love that most of us get from our own families," says Wesley Maat, a successful Wall Street analyst who volunteered with the coalition from 1989 to 1992. "They get a roof over their head, help finding jobs, counseling, literacy training, even something as basic as budgeting for meals. Many of them are used to going from one fast food meal to the next. What Ben provides them sounds elemental, but it is the bridge that helps a lot of families survive." In all, 70 percent of families that pass through the Coalition succeed in escaping poverty and homelessness.

The program, which is completely nondenominational but nevertheless based on faith in God, has been copied in several states, and was picked by IBM as one of the six exemplary charity programs in the country. Beltzer serves as the Coalition's executive director and chief operating officer, which means, as he puts it, "that I go down and clean bathrooms whenever it's needed." Beltzer also likes to bake cakes for the frequent celebrations of families leaving the program in solid shape. "Ben and his wife Patsy have had a lot of struggles in their lives, and that helps them extend to others in a compassionate way," says Wesley Maat. "Ben has hardly glided through life, and his past troubles serve to make his ministry more effective. His empathy for the people he helps is a quality that cannot be minimized."

Beltzer agrees that his time in the abyss has led to his success today. "I look back and I have to conclude that what happened to me was God's way of telling me how to help other people," he says. "That may be the most important lesson that I learned: when something like this happens, don't turn away from God. Move closer to Him." Had he not experienced horrendous loss and total dejection, Beltzer would not be able to share his hard-earned wisdom with those who need him. Consequently, hundreds and hundreds of people would not have the benefit of his extraordinary counsel. "What Ben brings to the table is hope," says Wesley Maat. "And that is an absolutely priceless gift to give."

The payoff for Beltzer, he insists, is spending time with the people who come to him for help. People who are kicking drugs, overcoming abuse, fighting off demons every day. People who get up at 4:00 a.m., take two bus trips, put their kids in daycare, and go to work, and then turn around at the end of the day and do it all in reverse. People who need an arm around their shoulders, just like Beltzer did. "These are the marginal people, the cast-offs from society, but they are some of the greatest, most courageous people I have ever met," he says. "I learn so much from them about courage, about faith, about how to live my life. I can honestly say that I have never been happier than I am today."

It is a wonderful life, indeed.

TIPS FOR TOUGH TIMES

The Ben Beltzer Story

What is defeat? Nothing but education; nothing but the first step to something better.

Wendell Phillips

en Beltzer thought he had a pretty good handle on how things worked, but that was before he lost all hope and decided to kill himself. On the other side of his ordeal—which, thankfully, he survived—was a truer and more meaningful picture of the world. That profound enlightenment could only be attained through the crucible of Beltzer's complete failure. The reason that, today, he is "the happiest I've ever been" is because of what he learned when he was broke and suicidal.

Beltzer is living proof that failure can be a positive, even spiritual experience. The business debacle that sent him spiraling all the way to the welfare line enabled him to see a real need that he was uniquely qualified to address. What's more, the struggles and hardships he endured made him a better, more empathetic person—and consequently a more effective minister. When he talks to people about hope, about courage, and believing in themselves, he draws from a deep well of experience. And experience is the best training tool there is.

1. **Failure Is a Test of Faith, Not a Reason to Give It Up** When his world crumbled around him, it would have been easy for Beltzer to totally abandon the most important thing in his life—his faith. In fact, he came within seconds of doing just that. But because he didn't, he realized that adversity is an opportunity to reaffirm your faith, not a convenient excuse to give it up. *In times of trouble, don't turn away from your deepest core beliefs; turn toward them and embrace them because you'll need them like never before.*

2. **Look for Lessons in Your Suffering** Failure truly is an education unlike any other. No book can convey the insight that a setback conveys; no teacher can illuminate what's meaningful quite like a catastrophe can. In Beltzer's case, his time on welfare lines opened his eyes to the plight of people he had previously ignored. It showed that his ministries had been incomplete and even half-hearted. It taught him things about himself he otherwise might have never known. *Look at failure as a sort of a cosmic classroom exercise, one that teaches you invaluable lessons you can't learn at Harvard or Yale.*

3. **Everybody Needs a Little Help Sometimes** The idea that anyone can make his or her way through life without a helping hand now and then defies all logic. Whether it's a financial gift to help you get back on your feet or a simple pat on the back to boost your confidence, assis-

tance from those around you is a crucial component of success. Pride should never stand in the way of accepting help from those who care about you. Beltzer had never needed much help in his life, until all of a sudden everything fell apart. That was when his friends stepped in and literally saved his life. These friends believed in Beltzer, and helped him believe in himself; now Beltzer has made it his mission to help others believe in themselves. *Don't be afraid to seek support from friends when you need it, even if all you need is an encouraging word.*

6 A FAMILY AFFAIR

The Kathy Garver Story

It took some failures and setbacks to make me realize exactly what I needed to do. And that was follow my heart.

Kathy Garver

It happened on a tennis court, on a perfect afternoon in Palm Springs. After years of looking for it in all the wrong places, of nearly despairing that it would ever happen, of almost forgetting that it was what she wanted most of all, suddenly there it was, on of all places a tennis court. And from that perfect day forward, Kathy Garver's life was never the same again.

The path that Garver took to finally get to that tennis court was a long and challenging one indeed. Along the way there were countless detours, a few wrong turns, and many unnecessary delays. Part of the problem was that Garver lost sight of exactly where she was going. She ignored what her heart was telling her to do. That is how people pass whole lifetimes of pain and unhappiness—they ignore what's in their hearts, what matters most to them. Kathy Garver nearly made that terrible mistake.

For years and years, she was certain of the direction she chose—and who could blame her? The daughter of an architect contractor and a nurse, she took dancing and singing lessons as a little girl and discovered she was a natural. "I really liked being in front of crowds," says Garver. "I would dance at these recitals and that was one of my favorite things to do. I remember one we did at the Shrine Auditorium in Los Angeles, all these tiny, tiny kids on this great big stage. I still have the outfit I wore in that one." Her mother didn't push young Kathy into show business, but she fully supported her interest in performing, and drove her to all of her lessons. When Kathy was still a wee little thing, she landed a part in Charles Laughton's dark classic, *Night of the Hunter*. The hobby was now a profession, and a dream had been born.

Garver didn't act all that much in her teens, but she did study theater arts as an undergraduate at UCLA. Then her agent told her about a new TV show in the works, a warm and cuddly sitcom called "Family Affair." The lead roles had already been cast: veteran Brian Keith would play a wealthy bachelor, and Sebastian Cabot would be his trusty valet. Two adorable child actors—Johnny Whitaker and Annisa Jones—were already signed on as his young niece and nephew. One role remained to be cast: Cissy, the teenaged niece. Garver was perfect for the part, except for one thing: all the actors already on board were blond, and she had long brown hair. "So my mom came over to the sorority house where I lived and sprayed my hair with this gold stuff so it looked blonde," Garver recalls with a laugh. "And I'm sitting at the audition and the guy says, 'What's wrong with your hair, it's turning green!' " She got the part anyway.

Just like that, Garver was a regular on a prime time TV show. In that first season of "Family Affair," she filmed a whopping 39 episodes. "I loved it," Garver says. "It was just very exciting, very cool. I had a lot of fun taping the shows." She was only a teenager, and already her dream of becoming a famous actress had been realized.

But then something strange happened, not long after the show aired on CBS and became an instant hit. Garver noticed that her personality had changed. "I was always this friendly, outgoing, cheerleading person," she says. "But when people began recognizing me on the street and asking me for my autograph, I couldn't understand it. I wondered, 'What is wrong with these people? Why are all these people clustering around me?' I withdrew a little bit. You could say I was not 100 percent comfortable with fame." One day, she appeared on a talk show, and the host started a question by saying, "Well, you're really successful." Garver thought to herself, "I am? Oh, gee, I guess I am." Up until that moment, she says, "it had never, ever occurred to me that I was successful. I needed someone to actually tell me that I was, because I did not feel successful at all."

•••

It was the first hint of trouble in paradise, but not, by far, the last. While starring in "Family Affair," Garver dated a man whose best friend was an emergency room doctor. "And this man could not believe that I made more money than him," remembers Garver. "He was this ER doctor, and here I was a young actress making more than him. He kept saying, 'I can't believe it, I can't believe it.' He certainly was not pleased." Vastly out-earning all of her friends was strange and unsettling for Garver, who was shocked by the jealousy and resentment her celebrity could cause. She learned another hard lesson toward the end of her run on "Family Affair," when her business manager stole money from her. Now she realized she could not trust even those closest to her.

The show was cancelled after five successful seasons, giving way to edgier fare like "All in the Family." Garver, however, figured she was just getting started as a serious actress. She agreed to star in a musical version of "Family Affair" in Israel, and embarked on this latest adventure with great expectations. But once again she encountered the ugly side of show business. First, the other actors in the show resented her for making much more money than they did. Then a producer who promised her $3000 for a photo shoot did not come through with the money. "He was supposed to meet me to pay me, and he never came to the appointed place," says Garver. "I called him and said, 'Look, I'm leaving Israel, so you're going to have to meet me at the airport to pay me.' And he agreed to meet me there, but he never showed up." Garver can still summon the devastation she felt. "I remember standing in the airport crying my eyes out," she says. "How could someone promise you something and then not come through? I was really destroyed by that. Destroyed and disillusioned."

She would suffer another blow when her young costar on "Family Affair," Annisa Jones, died of a drug overdose 3 years after the show's cancellation. The little pigtailed girl who played Buffy and cuddled Mrs. Beasley was dead at the age of 18, done in by drugs and depression. "I could see that she was unhappy," says Garver. "I heard she was taking drugs after the show, and I knew that she never wanted to get back into show business. Her experience with "Family Affair" had not been a good one. But still I never imagined that she would do what she did. It was very, very difficult for me to handle that." Part of the problem, says Garver, "is that child actors are catered to, depriving them of valuable life skills. You have parents and agents who set up auditions, sign the contracts, do everything, and all you're supposed to do is show up. And then, somehow, you're supposed to make the transition from child actor to grown-up, and you're simply not prepared. You're used to just showing up."

There were other problems, too. For one thing, Garver couldn't shake the feeling that she had not earned her celebrity. "I didn't feel worthy of it," she recalls. "I felt that I should study acting more." So she packed her bags and flew to London to bone up on Shakespeare and other classics at the fabled Royal Academy of Dramatic Arts. Professionally, it was a wonderful experience, but Garver, still only in her early 20s, had a hard time being away from her friends and family. "I learned a lot, but I was very, very lonely," she says. "I was far away from home and I was all by myself." When she returned to the United States, "I expected to be welcomed as this serious actress," she says. "But it didn't work out quite like that. There weren't many film or TV jobs waiting for me." Instead, Garver hit the road and performed in plays on the dinner theater circuit. The midwest, the southeast, Texas, Florida—Garver traveled all over the country doing what she loved best: acting. So why was she so miserable all the time? "Once again, I was very lonely," she says. "I enjoyed the plays, I liked traveling, but at the end of the day I was all alone. I wound up going everywhere with my dog, Daisy, this cute cockerspaniel. She was my constant companion, and I even had it stipulated in my contract that I could take my dog."

But Daisy wasn't always enough to dispel the emptiness Garver felt inside. "It was this hollow feeling," she says. "I dated guys here and there, and I'd go out with my friends, but for the most part I was by myself. It was not a very happy time for me." Garver even bought a wonderful home in Sherman Oaks, California. Three bedrooms, two baths, beautiful view: everything a young and promising actress could hope for. Well, almost everything. "I was in that big house all alone," she says. "I was lonelier than ever." Garver was coming up on 30 now, and the acting jobs were farther and fewer between. "I would sleep until 10:00 in the morning, go out and look for work, go to the gym, make some calls, straighten up around the house, and that was about it," she says. "In those days we didn't even have the computers, so there was no Internet to keep me busy."

Being alone was becoming a theme in Garver's life. A psychologist she dated came over to her house and was taken aback by the paintings on the walls. "He said, 'Kathy, have you ever really looked at these paintings? They are all of lone figures.' And I looked at them and suddenly I realized that he was right. Some of the paintings I had drawn myself, others I had purchased, but they all depicted lone, solitary figures. I had never realized that."

The worst moment came one lonely night, when Garver sat by herself watching a movie on TV. It was *The Old Man and the Sea*, starring Spencer Tracy. Based on an Ernest Hemingway novel, it told the story of an old fisherman who wages a battle against a big fish for several long days out on the desolate sea. "And I identified with the fisherman," says Garver. "I was sitting there watching this movie all alone, and suddenly I burst into tears. I couldn't believe that this was what my life had become. I was terribly lonely."

● ● ●

That's when Garver took a good, hard look at her situation and figured out what was wrong. "I said to myself, 'You're in your 30s, so why don't you have a baby yet?'" says Garver. "'Why aren't you married, and why don't you have a child?' The thing is, I always wanted a baby more than anything in my entire life.

From day 1, I loved my dolls. I had doll carriages, dollhouses, I fed my dolls, I changed them, I dressed them, the whole bit. That was my training to be a mother, because I wanted a baby more than anything. And it totally eluded me." She had one serious boyfriend, for 3 years, but that didn't work out. A couple of other suitors asked for her hand in marriage, but she turned them down. Nothing seemed quite right. Then, after years of being alone, "I started to think, 'I really want to be married, okay?' And that became my goal. At one point I was so desperate that I told myself, 'The next person that you meet, you are going to marry.' "

By then, Garver was in Palm Springs, fixing up a condo she had recently purchased. A friend asked her to sign up for a tennis tournament at a Palm Springs hotel, and Garver, a big tennis buff, said sure. "So I'm out there on the court practicing, and this big, handsome guy comes on, and I said to myself, 'Oh, there he is, the next person I meet—the man I'm going to marry.' That was the mindset I was in." The man, David Travis, noticed Garver's tennis prowess and walked right over. "He says, 'Oh, finally, a woman who can play tennis, I'm going to get married,' " says Garver. "And I just laughed to myself."

Turns out the smile on her face was there to stay. After the tournament, Garver and Travis went to dinner, and the next day she drove him to her home in Sherman Oaks. They began dating, and before long decided to make it official. Kathy Garver, lonely and miserable for so long, was alone no more. "My wedding day was the most exciting day of my life," she says. "I dreamed about it as a kid and it all came true. The long white dress, little flower girls, an archway of roses, this beautiful swan made out of ice. When I walked down the aisle and got to the end, I just let out this enormous sigh. Everyone just started laughing, but for me it was the culmination of so many years of being lonely. They were all finally over."

Garver and Travis, a music industry executive who later went into the software business, moved to northern California. Garver continued acting, commuting back and forth to Los Angeles. She was blissfully happy being married, but still, something was missing. "Now I'm coming up on 40 years old," she says. "David and I had put off having a baby because we were busy and getting used to each other, but then I put my foot down." Garver got pregnant and "loved every day, every minute of that experience," she says. "I would take walks, pat my stomach and say to my baby, 'I'm so happy you are here.' I was just thrilled every day to be pregnant. I was glowing." Finally, she welcomed a beautiful boy into the world. "He was gorgeous, beautiful, perfect," says Garver. "Holding him for the first time, I just let out another huge sigh."

Now she had what she always wanted: a husband, a baby, a family. No more late-night movies all alone, no more depressing pictures on the wall, no more missing pieces to the puzzle of her life. Garver had never stopped acting altogether; she had simply realized that it wasn't her main priority. Her early success as an actress seemed to set the direction she took, but as she matured she grew more and more disillusioned with show business. She was tired of waiting for roles to open up, for jobs to come to her. It was no way to live, and besides, she had a family now. She made a decision: acting was no longer the principle focus in her life.

And that's when the work really started pouring in. "I thought that after the baby was born I would not be very active," says Garver. "Instead I was as busy as ever, if not busier." Garver did a little of everything: she recorded voice-overs, she joined a friend in a toy company called Edutainment for Kids, she wrote songs, she produced audio books. "After Reid, I gravitated toward the children's market," she explains. "Everything I did was family-oriented. And that kept me amazingly busy. Suddenly I was producing things, making things happen instead of waiting for the phone to ring. And that was very important, particularly to a former child actress. I went out and did all these things for myself. Now I'm so busy I have to write these lists just so I know where I'm supposed to go."

Shifting the focus to her personal needs transformed Garver's professional career. The problem had never been that she wasn't talented or hard-working enough, it had simply been that she was killing herself in pursuit of the wrong goal. Yes, she enjoyed acting and longed for a steady stream of jobs. But her real goal, her real *dream*, was to be a mother, to have a family. That was what she wanted from the very beginning, but somehow it got pushed aside, and even forgotten altogether. Perhaps there was a feeling that motherhood was not, by itself, a suitable ambition. And perhaps Garver would not have been happy just being a mother while her yearning to act went unfulfilled. But ignoring the call of her heart undoubtedly caused Garver years of pain and frustration. "It took me a while to realize that the reason I was so lonely was that I wasn't going after my real dream, which was to be married and have a baby," says Garver. "And finally I told myself, 'Okay, then go out and get married and have a kid. What are you waiting for?' That was an important moment. It took some failures and setbacks to make me realize exactly what I needed to do. And that was follow my heart."

Now Kathy Garver has come full circle. Recently she produced and directed a little play called *Charlie and the Chocolate Factory*, staged at an elementary school in her hometown and featuring none other than her young son, Reid. "He's a very creative child," she says. "At first he was shy and reticent about acting, but then I gave him a little part in this project I was doing, and that kind of spurned him on. I'm certainly not going to push him, but he does have an agent and he may go out on interviews."

Young Reid will surely get great acting tips from his mother, but the most useful piece of advice she'll give him may be this: "Listen to your heart. You cannot be fulfilled just by being in show business. The happiest people are the ones who combine the love of what they do with the love of their life. Go after what your heart tells you to, and never, never, ever give up."

It is a lesson Kathy Garver learned well, and one that she is thankful for every day. "I am always happy when I get up in the morning now," she says. "Sometimes I'll just be sitting in the den with my husband and my son, and I will stop reading or whatever I'm doing and just look at them, and then I will say, 'You know, guys, I am just so happy right now. I can't think of any place in the world I'd rather be at this moment than right here, with the two of you.' "

TIPS FOR TOUGH TIMES

The Kathy Garver Story

Defeat strips away false values and makes you realize what you really want. It stops you from chasing butterflies and puts you to work digging gold.

William Moulton Marston

Some failures announce themselves loudly and unequivocally; others arrive in the quiet of evenings spent all alone at home. Kathy Garver realized she was miserable while watching a movie in the middle of the night, a moment that made her see that something was terribly wrong with her life. She wasn't a resounding failure in the traditional sense of the word; rather, she was someone who was simply chasing the wrong goal. It took the "failure" of her loneliness to clear the way for the most important realization of her life.

How many people spend years and years laboring under a misdefinition of "success"? What if Kathy Garver had landed juicy acting roles and even become a famous celebrity? Might she have even further delayed the one thing that could make her truly happy? In a way, the struggles she endured trying to make it in show business were the very best things that could have happened to her. They brought her to a state of true self-awareness, further proof of the uncanny power of failure.

1. **Don't Let Others Define Success for You** Kathy Garver got into acting as a little girl, and liked it well enough. Needless to say, she was also very good at it, and starred on one of the most popular sitcoms of all time. But even then, when others would tell her she was a huge success, Garver never thought of herself in those terms. Something about the business made her uneasy and left her unfulfilled, even though it took her years to finally admit that to herself. For too long, she simply relied on someone else's definition of a success. *Figure out for yourself what success means because what works for someone else might leave you feeling cold.*

2. **Ask Yourself: Did I Fail My Goal or Did My Goal Fail Me?** Pursuing a career in acting was not only the natural thing for Garver to do, but also a perfectly healthy and positive endeavor. The problem was that by itself, it was not a sufficient goal for Garver. No acting role could ever bring her the peace of mind she craved; no amount of fame or fortune could make her feel successful inside. Only after she found herself alone and miserable did she tear apart the façade of her life and focus on what she knew deep down to be true—the thing she wanted more than anything else was to be married and have a family. *False expectations can destroy any chance we*

have at happiness; take the blinders off and redirect yourself toward the goal that will really fulfill you.

3. **How Do I Know What My True Goal Is? Listen to Your Heart** Life would be easy if we all held the key to our happiness right from the start. But the fact is that self-awareness can require painful introspection, something many people are wary to undertake. Failure, of course, forces us to be introspective, but it shouldn't take calamity to make us look within. Imagine going through life without really asking yourself what it is that makes life special for you? *Take the time to shed the protective armor you wear every day because that's the only way you can hear what your heart is telling you.*

7 THE CHIPS ARE NEVER DOWN

The Wally Amos Story

If you give up when things go wrong, you lose for sure. But if you hang in there, something good might happen. That's just common sense.

Wally Amos

The most powerful man in the free world confirmed it—Wally Amos was a huge success. It was 1986, and President Ronald Reagan presented Amos with an Award for Entrepreneurial Excellence, one of the first such awards ever given by the Commander-in-Chief. By then, Amos—who in 1975 opened the first gourmet cookie store in the country, Famous Amos—had been hailed as one of the "Hot New Rich" on the cover of *TIME*, and appeared on TV and in magazines in his trademark Panama hat and Hawaiian shirt, both of which were destined for the Smithsonian Institute. His company's revenues were in the millions, and his chocolate chip cookies were popular from Sunset Boulevard to Singapore. By all observable yardsticks, Wally Amos was a classic American success story. But on the day in 1986 when he shook the President's hand, Amos knew something about his company that no one else knew.

Famous Amos was falling apart.

In fact, Amos was only 2 years away from losing all equity in the company, and only 3 years away from cutting his ties to it altogether. "There were cracks in the foundation of Famous Amos from the very first minute I opened my doors," says the charismatic Amos from his home in Hawaii. "My first mistake was believing that I knew everything about my business, and closing my mind to other people who knew a lot more than I did. That was the beginning of my downfall." Before his precipitous slide was through, Amos had lost his home, his passion for cookies, even the rights to use his own name. But one thing he never lost was the sunny disposition that made him a star in the first place. He started a second cookie company, saw it struggle, then started a *third* company, Uncle Wally's, which today is a sound and robust business venture. His is the classic rags-to-riches and back-to-rags and then *back*-to-riches story, a dizzying journey that gives him a unique perspective on traditional notions of success and failure. "What I discovered is that you can never get too emotional, no matter what is happening around you," says Amos, who this year celebrates an amazing 25 years in the baking business. "People have this idea that there are moments when you should feel elated, and moments when you should feel devastated. But life is a continuum: sometimes it's up, sometimes it's down, sometimes it's sideways. At the depths, it's heading up. And at the peaks, it's going down. Life is a ride, so just hold on and enjoy it as much as you can."

Amos never had a grand plan to become a cookie magnate. Growing up in Tallahassee, Florida, he lacked the confidence to even fathom such grandiose ideas. "I didn't have a lot of self-esteem," says Amos. "I was this skinny little kid, intimidated by my mother, and being raised in Florida at the height of segregation. It was a very negative environment, and not conducive to having any kind of aspirations about my life." But it was during his childhood that he experienced the seminal moment of his life: the day he first tasted his Aunt Della's legendary chocolate chip cookies. "Oh, they were so wonderful, the best I ever had in my life," he recalls. "When the cookie jar was empty, I'd put on a long face and my Aunt Della would go and bake some more." Later, when Amos dropped out of high school and joined the Air Force, his aunt would mail him tins filled with her fragrant cookies. "I'd make the mistake of opening them in a roomful of guys," he says. "The whole damn box would be gone in a few seconds."

•••

After the Air Force, Amos got his GED degree and worked as a manager at Saks Fifth Avenue in Manhattan, then moved to the mailroom at the William Morris talent agency. "I made agent in less than a year," says Amos, who in his 7 years in the company carved out a successful niche in the music industry, nurturing a young Simon and Garfunkle and booking the Supremes on their very first tour. Bored with the business and doubtful he could advance any further at William Morris, Amos moved to Los Angeles and started his own management company, signing Hugh Masakele, a well-known South African trumpeter. The move led to his first scary brush with adversity. No sooner had he landed in Hollywood than his client dumped him. "All of a sudden my life is unraveling," remembers Amos, who had two children at the time, the youngest two months old. "We were staying in a home that I figured my company would subsidize, and now all that was out the window. It was a very shaky time, but even then I did not fall apart."

With the help of some friends, Amos got back on his feet as a personal manager. But there would be more bad breaks—literally. One client fell off a ladder and broke his ankle, others lost their recording contracts, still others failed to pay Amos the commissions they owed him. But Amos always maintained the even keel that has seen him through a quarter century of setbacks. "You have got to hang in there when you confront adversity," he says. "Because things can change in a heartbeat. In a single instant, something could come into your life that you never dreamed would happen, and turn everything around for you. The key is to stay in the game. If you give up when things go wrong, you lose for sure. But if you hang in there, something good might happen. That's just common sense."

Amos spent 7 years as a personal manager before once again feeling the itch to try something different. That's when the memory of Aunt Della's cookies came in handy. Years earlier, Amos had begun baking his own cookies, based on his aunt's loving recipes. "I'd go to meetings and break out the cookies and everyone would have them before discussing anything," he says. "People loved them so much, they would see me and, even before they said hello, they'd say, 'Hey, man, where are my cookies?' I had a small but very loyal following for my chocolate chip cookies." One day, a friend suggested they open a store that sold Amos's creations. Amos turned to some show business friends—Marvin Gaye and Helen Reddy among them—and scraped together the $25,000 he needed to open the store. On March 10, 1975, in a 1400-square-foot space at 7181 Sunset Boulevard in Los Angeles, he opened Famous Amos, the country's first gourmet cookie store. The previous day, he had invited 2500 media types to a prelaunch party, hoping to generate some word-of-mouth business in lieu of his nonexistent advertising budget. "That first morning," he says, "we had people standing in line to get in."

The key to his cookies? "My secret was the same as Aunt Della's secret, and that was that she put everything she had into making them," says Amos. "She made them with love and with passion, and so did I. And that showed up on the balance sheet." It also helped that Amos was a masterful promoter. Known for his natty Panama hat, his bushy beard, and his beaming, ever-present smile, Amos was shrewd enough to put his image on a big sign outside his store, and to use his distinctive personality as his primary marketing tool. When people walked into his first store, they encountered Famous Amos himself, playing a kazoo and offering them "free smells" of his magical cookies. After he expanded to other stores and started selling his cookies in supermarkets, he remained the company's most valuable asset, the instantly recognizable face behind the irresistible cookie. "I was on the cover of *TIME*, I was in *PEOPLE* magazine, I was everywhere," he says. "People would see me and assume that the company was this huge success."

In fact, Amos's remarkable ability to connect with the public became a smokescreen that hid the company's flaws. "The promotion of the business was so much bigger than the business itself," he says. "The whole thing was based on the image I had created. But there was no good structure or management team in place." Amos knew going in that he didn't have formal business training, that he was more of a front man than a real entrepreneur. But no bona fide businesspeople believed in his venture and came aboard, and Amos was forced to handle all his business affairs himself. "People were talking about how great Famous Amos was and I got sucked in by it. Your head gets big, your ego grows, and then you start thinking that you can do things that before you *knew* you couldn't do." Amos saw the signs that he was in way over his head, but he kept any apprehensions he had to himself. On the day that Famous Amos cookies went on sale at Bloomingdale's with a huge fanfare, Amos left the splashy event to go see his investment banker. "I was $15,000 overdrawn in my checking account," he says. "But I didn't tell anyone these things because I didn't want anyone to know the company wasn't sound."

Eventually, Famous Amos expanded to 65 stores. The cookies were distributed worldwide through 8500 retail outlets. Annual sales reached a peak of $11 million. It was, at least on the outside, an unqualified success story. But the year that President Reagan hailed Amos as an entrepreneurial hero, his company was beginning to come apart at the seams. In 1988 it lost $2.5 million. Spread too thin without qualified management in place, Amos was forced to sell a portion of his ownership in the company to outside partners, reducing his interest in Famous Amos to 17 percent. Three more investment groups were eventually brought in, and Amos handed over his last bit of ownership in 1988. All he had left was an employment agreement to promote his cookies, and he gave that up when the final venture capital group came aboard in 1989. "The day I left, my monthly income dropped to zero," says Amos. "I had to start doing lectures and dipping into savings and things like that to get by. Soon I was borrowing money from friends just to stay alive."

●●●

By then, Amos knew enough not to panic as his world collapsed. The underpinnings of his company may have been weak, but his spiritual foundation was as strong as ever. "It has never made much sense to me to be depressed," he says. "I am not a cookie, and I am not a store—I am a child of God. By the time I lost Famous Amos, I was relatively strong inside, and I knew that I would be okay." Amos may not have been able to stop the fiscal hemorrhaging that was killing his business, but he could control the way he felt about it. "People expect you to be devastated or discouraged, but that is just a mindset. That's not the way life is supposed to be lived. I create the circumstances in which my life is lived, not everybody else. Heck, the one thing I *could* control through all of that was my attitude. And if you can control your attitude, you control everything."

But Amos was human, after all, and he did feel the sting of losing the company he created. He stopped wearing his favorite hats, and shaved off his well-known beard. He even quit baking chocolate chip cookies for himself. "I just didn't want to do that anymore," he recalls. "It was a time of purging, of transition, of change. But it was insanity to stop baking cookies because I love them so much. I also realized that I had built up this incredible relationship with my customers, so why not capitalize on that? Why just throw it all away?"

And so Amos started his second company, one that sold chocolate chip macadamia nut cookies (and two plush stuffed dolls) under the name Wally Amos Presents. Before long, the people who owned Famous Amos sued him for trademark infringement. The lawsuit dragged on for 19 months, but Amos didn't wait until it was over to change the name of his company to the purposefully defiant Uncle Noname. He brought to these endeavors the same marketing prowess that had made him a nationally known celebrity, yet he still lacked the management skills and the resources to make them a success. His finances were so tight that he fell 15 months behind on his mortgage. One day, while he was promoting his cookies at an event in Utah, Amos was told that his repossessed house had been sold at auction. It was the latest crisis to challenge the perpetually positive Amos, and the latest chance for him to test his theory of survival. "The one thing I have always had throughout my adult life is the ability to focus on answers and solutions," he explains. "How else are you going to come out of a crisis? If you only focus on the problem, it gets bigger."

Amos likens facing adversity to being mired in quicksand. "If you start flailing about, you'll go down like a rock. But if you just stay still, if you take really slight breaths, if you just stay cool and survey the area, you're going to last a lot longer. And then someone might come along and save you, or you might spot a branch that you can grab and pull yourself out. Believe me, if you are only focused on being in quicksand and thinking you're going to die, then you will die. It's all about where you focus your attention."

That was the attitude that allowed Amos to weather one of his worst storms: the bankruptcy of Uncle Noname in 1997. Here he was, a pioneer in the world of gourmet cookies and marketing strategies, totally bankrupt and unable even to use his own name. That might have been enough to drive him out of the baking business once and for all, but Amos simply treated it as another dip in the roller-coaster ride of life. "We came out of bankruptcy with no capital, with a crippled company, with nothing," he says. "But I was determined to correct the mistakes I had made in the past." This time around, Amos partnered with Lou Avignone, named him president and CEO, and allowed him to run the company. He also switched from making cookies—by then a crowded market—to making sugar-free and fat-free muffins. Uncle Noname was back on its feet, better and healthier than ever. "The whole experience of losing Famous Amos and going into bankruptcy really strengthened me," says Amos. "And it strengthened the company. What we had in place now was a strong management team. And we are now a very viable business."

There was more good news on the horizon. In 1999, Keebler, the company that purchased Famous Amos, approached Amos to resume his role in promoting his chocolate chip cookies. Though he was in no position to negotiate, Amos insisted that Keebler improve the quality of the cookies, and return to him the right to use his name to promote his own company. Keebler agreed, and Uncle Noname became Uncle Wally. "Hey, at least I got *half* my name back," Amos says with a laugh.

His latest product may not be connecting with the public as quickly as his cookies did, but Amos thinks that Uncle Wally has an excellent chance to truly succeed. After all, it has something going for it that his previous companies didn't—a good business plan and solid management. And it has a spokesperson who is all the wiser thanks to the setbacks he endured. "I thank God for all those experiences, good and bad," he says. "It's like a mathematical equation: if you change one thing, you change the outcome. Hey, if you took out any of the stuff I went through, I might even be dead, who knows? There are no tough times, there are only opportunities to grow."

His contribution to the gourmet food industry is, indeed, enormous, but his lasting legacy may be as a positive thinker. Amos has written four books that brim with his infectious optimism: *The Famous Amos Story, The Power in You, Man with No Name*, and *Watermelon Magic*. He continues to lecture frequently, driven to convince as many people as he can that they possess the power to control their lives. "We have these negative belief systems in this country, where people think that they're supposed to give up when they face adversity. People are told, 'You can't do this, you can't do that, you might as well give up.' And that is just not so. People sell themselves short every day, they are crippled by a lack of self-esteem. I know, I went through it. And that is why my mission in life is helping people feel better about themselves. That is on the back of my business card."

Twenty-five years after he first burst into the public consciousness, Wally Amos hasn't lost his high-wattage smile. The Panama hat is gone, and the handsome face is clean-shaven now, but the smile, that incredible smile, is still bright enough to power some small towns. He started with nothing, made a fortune, lost it all, and rallied back, and through it all he learned something important about failure—indeed, about life. "Henry Ford said that failure is just an opportunity to begin again more intelligently," says Amos. "And, hey, it took Edison 10,000 tries to create the filament for the light bulb. If he had quit at 8000 or 9000, we'd all be sitting around in the dark. The whole concept of failure is all wrong, man. I mean, everything we do in life, we have to do for a first time. So how can you fail at something for which you had no training, something you never did before? Life is a process, life is a ride. If something goes wrong, just start over and you'll get it right."

And that, for Famous Amos, is the way the cookie crumbles.

TIPS FOR TOUGH TIMES

The Wally Amos Story

One is wasting life force every time he talks of failure, of hard luck, of troubles and trials, of past errors and mistakes. Let him turn his back on the past and face the light.

Orison S. Marden

There may not be a more positive thinker on the planet than Wally Amos. He bristles when people mention the word "failure" to him; he'd rather view those experiences as happy chances to get something right. To Amos, the stigma that attaches to failure in this country is a most unfortunate and worrisome thing. Had he dwelled on his own mistakes and let them sap his energy, he would not have been able to bounce back the way he did. And then the thousands of people that he helps feel good about themselves would have been deprived of his remarkable counsel.

The truth is that while Amos did "fail" once or twice and even occasionally felt discouraged, he quickly turned his setbacks into "opportunities to grow." Every error and misstep was a good thing, another brick added to his wall of knowledge. He proved that simply by viewing failure differently, it is possible to turn it into a positive event. His most effective resource was always his upbeat attitude. To beat yourself up

*because you fail at something is, to Wally Amos, a far, far
more destructive thing than to fail in the first place.*

1. **Accept What Happened and Move On** Wally Amos never let his
   setbacks overwhelm him. He was quick to acknowl-
   edge his failings, and even quicker to move on to the
   next thing. Once again, it's simply common sense to
   him: before you can figure out a solution, you have to
   honestly confront the nature of your problem. Losing
   his Famous Amos cookies was, Amos knew, a factor
   of his business inexperience. Rather than dwell on his
   terrible misfortune, he quickly came up with another
   line of cookies, and put himself in a position to eventually reclaim the use of his name. *Nothing can be
   gained from kidding yourself about the reason you failed
   or feeling unjustly victimized; you've got to face facts
   before you can face the future.*

2. **Always Stay Positive!** It's the oldest cliché in self-help liter-
   ature: positive thinking works wonders! It also happens to be the simple key to restructuring your life.
   Every situation can be viewed a number of ways; why
   not always choose to view them in the most positive
   light? What can possibly be gained from putting a
   negative spin on things? When times are particularly
   tough or trying, that's when a positive attitude comes
   in handiest. *When failure rears its ugly head, flip the
   script and welcome the chance to give it another go.*

3. **Don't Sell Yourself Short** We are capable of so much more than we give ourselves credit for. Consequently, we usually settle for less than what we can and should have. In particular, people who experience failure can suffer from bouts of crippling self-doubt. A little adversity can cause them to crumble and give in to the "inevitable." These self-imposed limits are totally arbitrary and, in essence, a cop-out. In fact, failure presents an opportunity to rise and prosper in ways you never dreamed. *Do not fold your tent at the first hint of trouble; know that we are all fully capable of surviving—and even thriving—in the teeth of the most terrible storm.*

8 THINKING BIG

The Rick Hvizdak Story

You become what you think you are. The attitude you develop is the most important ingredient in determining your level of success.

Rick Hvizdak

He was the first man on the first tee on the first day that the Olde Stonewall Golf Club opened for play. And it felt good. It felt good to be the lucky man to christen such a lovely place. It was a brisk spring day in North Sewickley, Pennsylvania, 40 miles northwest of Pittsburgh, and Rick Hvizdak, a brawny, bearded, cheerful man, took a driver out of his golf bag and got ready to hit his ball. Before him lay perhaps the most magnificent new golf course to be built in America in a decade, a breathtaking blend of cascading waterfalls, plunging ravines, rolling hills, huge limestone boulders, and, of course, a massive stone wall that is visible for miles. Millions and millions of dollars had been spent, 360 million pounds of rocks had been hauled in, and now this glorious stretch of earth was ready for golfers like Hvizdak— a decent player with a handicap around 22—to wage battle in the shadow of Olde Stonewall's medieval castle clubhouse.

Hvizdak took a deep breath and addressed his ball. Only a few years earlier, it didn't seem likely that he would find himself on any sort of golf course, much less an upscale layout like Olde

Stonewall. Only a few years earlier, he was unemployed, out of money, coming off a nasty divorce, and living off his credit cards. He had no college degree to fall back on, no special skills to help him find work. What's more, his former boss—his older brother William, a successful, millionaire businessman—had fired him after an argument, leading to an ugly and prolonged family feud. Hvizdak, then 32 years old, sat in his house and asked himself, "How am I going to get myself out of this mess?" Months passed without him coming up with an answer.

And yet here he was, on the first tee at Olde Stonewall, about to play some leisurely golf on a breathtaking piece of land. Hvizdak took a short backswing and powered his way through the ball, driving it straight down the middle of the fairway, a good 230 yards away. He smiled and felt a deep sense of satisfaction, and not just because his drive had been a doozy.

No, Rick Hvizdak felt good because he had built this course. He felt good because the course was his.

● ● ●

Needless to say, Hvizdak did come up with the answer to his puzzling question: "How am I going to get myself out of this mess?" But it's just as instrumental to look at how he got himself into it. Raised on a farm outside of Hillsville, Pennsylvania, he was, by his own admission, a poor and inattentive student in high school. "I'd stare out the window and daydream about things," says Hvizdak, the middle brother among five. "I like to say that I finished in the upper two-thirds of my class." But even back then, on those lazy high school days, Hvizdak knew what he wanted out of life. "At a fairly early age I knew that I wanted to be successful," he says. "I had ambitions. It wasn't greed, exactly, but I would see people who had nice things and I would think, 'If I work hard and think smart, I'll be able to have those things someday, too.' "

To that end, Hvizdak was a remarkably industrious young man. "I started working almost right away," he recalls. "I was 6 years old when I got my first job, helping my father, who was a carpenter. I would sand a lot of his moldings and plaques, after school, every night. He'd pay me a nickel an hour." At age 13, he got a job picking mushrooms in a mushroom mine. "I'd put on my coal-miner's helmet and go into this building where they had all these mushroom beds, and I'd stand in these beds and pick mushrooms and put them into my basket, all day." For that, he earned about $1.32 an hour, plus a four cents an hour bonus for anything over 32 lbs. an hour. The Hvizdaks of Hillsville weren't poor, but they weren't exactly well off either, and so the boys learned to earn. Working hard became as much a part of young Rick's life as eating and breathing. During his high school years, he held five different jobs, from picking mushrooms to pumping gas to selling milk. He was working as much as 40 hours a week while attending classes. "Never took a book home, though," he says. "Never had time to study."

That changed the day he graduated from high school. Someone gave him an intriguing graduation present: a copy of Dale Carnegie's seminal motivational book, *How to Win Friends and Influence People*. "It had a big, big influence on me," he says. "Positive thinking, inspirational messages—I just ate it up." Suddenly, his vague and inherent desire to succeed found a crystal-clear voice in Carnegie's can-do philosophies. Suddenly, Hvizdak had the fuel to power his drive. He has gone on to read more than 500 motivational books, and listen to over 100 inspirational audiotapes. "And I really believe," he says, "that all that information was implanted so deep down in my subconscious, the word failure was totally blocked out of my mind."

●●●

College was not a realistic option for Hvizdak, who despite his solid work ethic never did well in the classroom. Instead, he did what he did best: rolled up his sleeves and broke a sweat. He went to work on a dynamite crew, blasting and drilling in strip mines. After that he got into auto sales, peddled insurance, and even sold golf carts. "I thought I was a pretty good salesman," he says. "I worked long hours and I spent a lot of time thinking how I could sell the product, how I could make people buy what I was selling."

Then his brother Bill, older by 10 years, offered Hvizdak a job. The two weren't exceptionally close, since Bill left the farm when Rick was only 8. But now Bill had secured a license agreement to run the western Pennsylvania division of Record Data, a company that did title searches and loan appraisals for consumer finance companies, credit unions, and banks. Hvizdak started in the sales department, and in his 7 years at Record Data brought a bunch of clients to the business. "Hey, as far as I was concerned, I pretty much ran the business," he now says. "In my opinion, Bill did not manage that company right. He is one of the absolute worst persons at dealing with people I have ever seen. But it was his company, and I guess I sometimes failed to realize that he was the boss."

Hvizdak's 7 years at Record Data would not be happy ones. He and Bill just didn't get along, and often lapsed into adolescent behavior not atypical of warring brothers. "What Bill would do is try and humiliate me every chance he got," says Hvizdak. "He would say things that he thought were funny at my expense, making little comments, trying to downgrade me all the time. Demeaning-type things to make me look like an ass. I'm not sure he even realized he was doing it, but he was doing it." Hvizdak didn't like the way his brother treated him, the way he would play him for a fool in front of other people, the way he often criticized him in the presence of coworkers. "It hurt, but I'm a pretty tough-skinned guy," says Hvizdak. "I just put up with it for as long as I could. But then things got to a boiling point."

Things blew up on Hvizdak's 32d birthday. He and Bill went out to lunch to discuss a few work-related matters. Rick wanted a particular staff person fired; Bill refused. The argument grew heated, and moved back to Bill's office after lunch. Finally, Bill said, "Why don't you just get your ass out of here, you're fired!" And Rick responded, "No, I quit!" He threw the keys to his company car on the desk and stormed out. Sure, he had been fired twice before, but those were minor flare-ups compared to this humdinger of a fight. This time Hvizdak knew he was leaving Record Data for keeps. "And you know what? It felt great," he recalls. "It was time for me to move on, time to be my own boss, time to get out from my brother's shadow."

That initial euphoria, however, would soon wear off. Around the time that his own brother fired him, Hvizdak became enmeshed in a difficult divorce from his now ex-wife, who wound up with custody of their two sons. Just like that, Hvizdak had lost his job, his family, his balance in life. He retreated to his townhouse and sat out on his back deck, staring at the sky and asking himself, "How am I going to get myself out of this mess?" It was a major crossroad in his life, as much an opportunity to rise and succeed as an excuse to crash and burn. All the daydreams of his youth, all the credos in Carnegie's book—here was Hvizdak's chance to test his mettle, to practice what he preached, to truly discover what kind of stuff he was made of.

He had no money, and lived off his credit cards. He was a smoker and a drinker, fond of the nightlife and not exactly the healthiest guy on the block. He was out of a job and short on prospects, while the brother he thought was a poor businessman was thriving. By all objective measurements, he was in miserable shape. But that was not the way that Rick Hvizdak saw things. No, he saw himself as a raw mound of clay ready to be sculpted into a thing of beauty. And that's just what he set out to do.

He stopped drinking and smoking, and started going to the gym five nights a week. He stopped carousing with lots of different women, and settled on one steady girlfriend. He streamlined his lifestyle so that he could survive on roughly $1000 a month. And he immersed himself in motivational literature. Dozens and dozens of books and tapes, all with the same essential message—you can do whatever you set your mind on. Rick Hvizdak was brainwashing himself. "I really got heavy duty into the motivational books," he says. "No booze, no cigarettes, no partying, working out—I was getting ready to go to battle. I was like a warrior in training. I would even play inspirational music to get myself pumped up. I was really revving myself to go out and conquer the world."

And, every day, he asked himself the same question: How am I going to get myself out of this mess? "That first day that I was fired, I went home and sat in my Lay-Z-Boy recliner, and I asked myself that question. I simply thought and thought about the steps I had to take to dig myself out." Because he knew that he liked the vendor-management business and had done fairly well at it, he added a second part to his basic question: "What can I do to fundamentally change this business and make it better for our customers?" Every day, several times a day, he asked those questions of himself, and every day, several times a day, he drew a blank.

This went on for 6 months.

Still, Hvizdak did not panic. Yes, there were days when he wondered if he would ever get off that back porch, but those moments passed quickly, and he would always resume his methodical training regimen. And he kept reading his motivational books. Tony Robbins, Brian Tracy, Harvey McKay—you name it, Rick read it. He would write the most lucid and meaningful observations and insights into spiral notebooks, filling several notebooks that way. He would refer to them whenever he felt a little down to reinforce his belief in himself. To this day, he keeps those spiral notebooks on his desk. "I really, really believe that you become what you think about," he explains. "If you always think about doing more than is required, if you see yourself as an achiever, then you will be successful. The attitude you develop is the most important ingredient in determining your level of success. It's like they say: 'Don't let frustration stop your day, let determination move it.'"

There was no rock-bottom moment for Hvizdak: he was too busy compiling his notebooks to get too distraught. "I never needed Valium and had anxiety attacks or woke up sweating in the middle of the night," he says. "I was out of work for 6 months and I was really out of money, but I just never thought of myself as a failure. I thought of myself as a success waiting to happen. I felt confident, strong. I always felt that if you're not the steamroller, you're the road. And I was the steamroller. I felt I had the ability to create, run, and manage a business. And so what I was doing was getting ready to play with the big boys."

Hvizdak finally came up with an answer to the question that nagged him for months—he proposed a way for the real estate lending industry to share in the profits of the title and appraisal industry. He also developed software that made collecting loan and credit data much more efficient and paperless. Now all he had to do was sell his brilliant idea. Hvizdak hired a video crew, persuaded a local businessman to loan him his fancy office, and taped a 13-minute presentation. "Hello, I am Rick Hvizdak . . . and your business is being taken for granted," the tape began, with Rick pointing his finger defiantly right at viewers. He went on to pitch his idea and position himself as a hard-working upstart in the multibillion dollar real estate information industry. The night before he shot the video, Buster Douglas knocked out Mike Tyson in Tokyo, one of the greatest upsets in sports history. Hvizdak worked it into his presentation, likening himself to Buster, the amazing underdog who could. "It only goes to show that anyone with desire can win," Hvizdak intoned on the tape. "And my team and I have that desire."

Except, of course, there was no team yet. There was only Rick Hvizdak. And he was a guy who had been fired by his own brother. Who was going to buy his pitch? "I had a lot of friends who told me I was pipe dreaming," he says. "They'd say, 'You're crazy, you'll never get this, you might as well forget it.' The problem was they didn't see the concept that I saw, they didn't see the big picture." Undaunted, Hvizdak climbed into his tan Honda Accord and drove from Pennsylvania to Dallas, Texas, his videotape and accompanying notebook presentations in tow. In Dallas, he crashed the American Financial Services Association's annual convention, scanning crowded hotel ballrooms for name tags he recognized. When he spotted one CEO, Hvizdak swooped in and said, "Sir, I spent the last 6 months putting this presentation together, and I need 13 minutes of your time. And if you stay any longer than that, it will be because you want to." When the CEO agreed, Hvizdak took him to his 23rd-floor hotel room, where he had set up a VCR, and held his breath as his future teetered in the balance.

The CEO watched the tape and agreed to give Hvizdak a shot. "That was all I needed, a shot," he says. "A little daylight, a crack in the door. Now I was back in the game."

● ● ●

Hvizdak launched National Real Estate Loan Services. He ran it out of his townhouse for the first few weeks, then stocked a rented office with used furniture. In its first 24 months, it racked up some $4 million in sales. "I was profitable right out of the blocks," Hvizdak says. "I paid off all my credit cards within 6 months." What's more, his new software proved so successful at streamlining data, word of its usefulness soon filtered back to Rick's old boss, his brother Bill. "He called one day and wanted to buy our software," says Hvizdak. "I had 30 people doing the job that it took him 93 people to do. I told him I would sell it to him, but that he would have to give me a percentage of all the business he billed through it."

Not surprisingly, the deal did not go down. Rick and Bill had not gotten along when they worked together, and they would not get along now that they worked apart. "We're a little like Bobby and J. R. Ewing," says Hvizdak. "We have different philosophies on how things should be done." The only difference this time around was that younger brother Rick had the upper hand now.

Bill turned down his offer to pay a royalty to use the software, but eventually poached Hvizdak's programmer and tried to get the software for free. The case wound up in federal court, where a judge ordered the two brothers to merge their companies as a way to settle what he saw as a garden-variety family feud. "I didn't like the decision and I still don't," says Hvizdak. "But we merged our companies and I retained control of the whole thing."

The table had turned in a big way. The new company, National Real Estate Information Services, thrived, even as the relationship between the brothers got worse. Finally, Hvizdak fired his brother, and today the two don't talk. "We never reconciled, and I'm sorry about that, but we just don't see things the same way," says Hvizdak. "There was no way he was going to be happy reporting to me, and so I guess I'm not surprised it didn't work."

Hvizdak, on the other hand, was prospering. He built his own office building and moved his company in 2 years ago. He also gobbled up several acres of beautiful land in northern Pennsylvania, with the intent of joining with partners and building condos and houses. When that deal fell through, Hvizdak bought out his partners and found himself sitting on 268 acres of prime real estate. "I walked the property a bunch of times and I noticed all the woods, the waterfalls, the stream, the elevation changes, all this wonderful terrain," he says. "And one day after the deal fell through, I just said to myself, 'You know what? I'm going to build my own golf course right here.'"

People snickered, naturally. After all, Hvizdak wasn't even much of a golfer. Only a few years earlier he had joined the Pete Dye Golf Club in West Virginia, and learned the game on that course's remarkable property. But he felt his own 268 acres were comparably beautiful. What's more, he wasn't crazy about the country club way of life. "On my application, where it asked what college I attended, I wrote down, 'School of Hard Knocks,' " he recalls with a chuckle. "They didn't like that much and it almost cost me my membership." Hvizdak's idea was to create a majestic, upscale public golf course that average but dedicated golfers like him could enjoy. On December 31, 1996, he broke ground on Olde Stonewall Golf Club in North Sewickley.

Thanks to the brilliant architects he hired, Michael Hurdzan and Dana Fry, Olde Stonewall became an instant hit with golfers. It was recently ranked as one of the top 10 public golf courses in America by *Golf* magazine. It is an unqualified hit, an instant classic, a true field of dreams. "That first day we opened was a great, great day," says Hvizdak. "After 2½ years of crawling around in the mud, seeing this place come to life, it was just great to finally swing the club and get it going."

All the hundreds of motivational books had been right—he *could* do anything he set his mind to. His friends doubted him— heck, even his own brother derided him—but Hvizdak held firm to his belief: you're either the steamroller or you're the road. "The real lesson of it all is that you must never, ever give up," he says, invigorating the clichéd notion with palpable conviction. "Get your road map so you can see where you're going, and never, ever give up. When I got fired, I could have taken some other job just to make some money to live, but I didn't want to do that. I seized that opportunity to make a real difference in my life. It's not that being fired charged me up, it's that it made me realize I wanted to be a winner, not a loser. And I was going to do everything in my power to be a winner." A situation that others might have seen as abject failure struck Rick Hvizdak as the perfect chance to realize his dreams.

Today, he is a wealthy and hugely successful entrepreneur. And he's even improving as a golfer. "I generally shoot in the lower 90s," he admits. "But my best round ever is an 83 at Olde Stonewall last year. Not bad." The only problem these days is Hvizdak's cluttered schedule—the guy who built himself a golf club can only find the time to play about one round a month. "Yeah, I know, I'd like to get out a lot more, but I just don't make the time," he says. "I'm just too busy to play as much golf as I'd like."

Now how is he going to get himself out of that mess?

TIPS FOR TOUGH TIMES

The Rick Hvizdak Story

*Watch a man with scrutiny when his will is
crossed, and his desire disappointed. The quality
of spirit he reveals at that time will determine
the character of that man..*

Richard T. Williams

It's one thing to be fired from your job. It's another to be fired by your own brother. *It was the kind of rejection that made Rick Hvizdak take stock of himself, and from the outside looking in he seemed a failure in comparison to his rich and successful sibling. That, however, was the not way that Hvizdak saw himself. Instead of feeling victimized or otherwise vulnerable, Hvizdak recognized the freedom that failure bestowed on him. Liberated from a job he never really loved, Hvizdak was finally all systems go to chase his rightful dream.*

He might have never devised the plan that made him rich had he not spent months among the ranks of the unemployed. He might have never summoned the courage to go out on a limb had he not experienced the hardship of poverty. Hvizdak's response to adversity was a textbook example of grace under pressure. Rather than scratch and claw to get back to where he was, he used the opportunity to truly shoot for the stars.

1. **Failure Gives You Carte Blanche to Reinvent Yourself** Losing your job, and all your money, can easily lead to panic. In fact, such a situation calls for extreme calm. Hvizdak never despaired of escaping the mess he had created, even when he was down to his last dime. He rightly recognized that failure clears the decks, that losing your shirt means that all bets are off. Given the chance to redefine exactly who he was, Hvizdak aimed as high as he could—and wound up even higher! *Some people see failure as a reason to feel small, when in fact it is an invitation to think big.*

2. **Come Up with a Good Plan, Then Give It Everything You've Got** Hvizdak could have taken a salaried job to make ends meet; instead, he holed up in his house, devising a master plan to succeed. He very meticulously examined his strengths and weaknesses, and just as thoroughly looked at the industry he planned to infiltrate. Finally, after long weeks of strategizing, he came up with a solid plan—and executed that plan with uncanny confidence. He bucked the odds by being fully committed to his approach. *Use the downtime failure brings to carefully plot your comeback, and then give 110 percent to making it work.*

3. **Prepare, Prepare, Prepare** Hvizdak made sure he was ready when opportunity knocked. Not long after he was fired, he started going to the gym and got himself in

fighting shape. He kicked a couple of bad habits, and dedicated himself to achieving his goals. He also read dozens of self-help books, honing a positive attitude. Physically and mentally, Hvizdak was ready to be a winner. *Look at failure like a kick in the pants, and do whatever you have to do to make yourself stronger and better.*

9 FLYING HIGH

The John Starks Story

I wouldn't trade the struggles I went through for any-thing. They made me a very humble person, and they made me a better man.

John Starks

The court is some dirt in a neighbor's backyard, the rim a rusty tire iron. The backboard is made of splintered wood, and the net is nonexistent. The ball is old and badly scuffed up, barely orange anymore. But the kids—the kids! They are alive with the joy of playing basketball. Look at that little boy over there, the one who's buzzing around like a headless chicken. That's skinny little Johnny Starks, all of 7 years old—look at the joy on his face. And when the good-hearted neighbor sets up a trash can in front of the rim, the kids really go crazy, jumping off it and dunking the ball as if they're 7 feet tall. Look at little Johnny now, soaring toward the basket on the way to his very first dunk. Look at his face, at his expression—there is something other than joy there now, something deeper, more serious. Something is happening to him as he flies higher than he ever has before. "Sailing through the air like that, dunking the ball that first time, it was an unbelievable feeling," says Starks, now 34. "And when I dunked it, it was like someone flipped a switch inside me. That was the moment I knew that this was what I wanted to do."

Cut to Madison Square Garden in New York City, the most famous basketball arena in the world. It is 21 years after that first dunk, and John Starks is now a starting guard for the New York Knicks of the NBA. The Knicks are playing game 2 of the 1993 Eastern Conference Finals, with a berth in the World Championship Series at stake. Their competition: none other than the Chicago Bulls and Michael Jordan, only the best player this sport has ever seen. There is less than a minute to go in the game when Starks takes the ball along the right baseline and gets that familiar look on his cherubic face, the look that says he's going to ignite and do something truly special. Succeed or fail, John Starks is always a spectacle of energy and passion, a mesmerizing high-wire act performed without a net. Here he goes again, dribbling toward the basket, on a collision course with his determined defender—Michael Jordan.

Starks powers toward the basket and suddenly takes flight. Jordan and his teammate Horace Grant can see him coming, but before they can do much, Starks is rising high above them. He is only 6 feet 3 inches tall, relatively small for an NBA player, but he can jump, really jump, and this time he jumps as high as he ever has before. The ball is in his left hand, his weak hand, and his body seems to hang in the air, defying gravity. Just when it looks like he can't rise any higher, he does, another inch, maybe two, and then he does it—he thunderously dunks the ball, rocking the rim, stunning the crowd, leaving Jordan and Grant tangled helplessly below. The instant is electric, surreal—a "did I just see what I think I saw" sort of event. Years later, when the NBA celebrates its fiftieth anniversary, a clip of what was called "The Dunk" will be included in a highlight reel of the league's most glorious moments. Bill Russell blocking a shot, Kareem Abdul Jabbar skyhooking—and little Johnny Starks dunking over Michael Jordan. "People still come up to me and ask about that play" says Starks. "They sometimes get the people confused, but they always remember the dunk. I know I won't ever forget it myself."

Between the two dunks—the first one on the dirt court in a neighbor's backyard in Tulsa, Oklahoma, and the furious one in Madison Square Garden over Michael Jordan—there is a story of setbacks and frustrations, of near misses and bad breaks, and ultimately of heart and perseverance. The story explains how John Starks rose above his limitations, drew strength from his failures, and never, ever surrendered his dream, on the way to an unlikely and inspirational career. "I've seen some players come and go who had more talent," Dave Checketts, President of Madison Square Garden, once said. "But they didn't play as hard, they didn't work as hard, and they didn't care as much as John does."

●●●

The first setback came early, when Starks was only 3 years old. That was the year his father picked up and left the family. Luckily, John had two strong women to raise him in a hard-scrabble section of Tulsa—his mother Irene and his grandmother Callie West. He also had basketball, the thing that lit his youthful fire. "It has always been a big part of my life," says Starks. "Every young man growing up and playing in the playgrounds wants to make it to the NBA one day. I always had that fantasy of making something of myself and succeeding as a basketball player." After long days on his neighbor's dirt court, John would come back home and tune in basketball games on TV. "Watching the great players like Dr. J and Kareem, I really responded to the way they played the game, the passion and excitement they brought to it. That kind of intensity was instilled in me from a very early age."

But Starks was never wildly talented, and so his road to the NBA was fraught with potholes and detours. Undersized in high school, he quit the team after the coach benched him in favor of transfers from another school. "That turned me off to playing team basketball," Starks says. "But it did not turn me off to playing the game. I was always off working by myself, shooting and getting better." Persuaded by his buddies to rejoin the squad, he became the starting point guard in his senior year. His quick temper and rebellious streak, however, led him to leave the team again after a disagreement with the coach.

Things didn't go any more smoothly after he left high school. He shot up several inches and developed a muscular physique, but for 2 years no one offered him a basketball scholarship. So he found himself at Tulsa Junior College, taking a few classes and trying to fit in. "I was always struggling to find a spot for myself somewhere," he says. "I was just trying to hook up with some basketball program somewhere. It was very frustrating, but I never gave up. I hung in there. The thing is, I always believed I was good enough to compete against the college players. When I played in tournaments against them, I always did okay, and so I kept thinking that it was just a matter of finding a spot."

Finding that spot, however, was not an easy thing to do. Some high school players are courted by fawning college coaches. But no one ever fawned over John Starks. At one point, he took a job bagging groceries at a Safeway supermarket in Tulsa to make ends meet while he figured out which college program he'd try and crash next. At an age when other players were honing their skills in big college games and inching closer to their NBA dreams, Starks was stuffing bottles of Draino into paper bags for minimum wage. "I worked there for the money, but I didn't let it get me too down," he says. "When I wasn't at Safeway you could always find me at the gym. No matter what else was going on in my life, I was always working out, improving my game. I practically lived at the gym because I was determined to make something happen."

He got his chance when a scout from Oklahoma Junior College saw him playing in an intramural basketball game at Tulsa Junior. It didn't matter to Starks that he was playing against regular students with rusty skills and limited athleticism. His competitiveness has only one speed—overdrive. "I guess I kind of dominated those students," he says sheepishly. "And then the coach's son from Oklahoma Junior came to watch me play, and right away he said I should come over and try out."

Offered the chance to win a partial scholarship, Starks walked into the gym at Oklahoma Junior and saw a knee-weakening sight: 100 hungry players all vying for three or four spots on the basketball team. It was the kind of long odds that Starks would face again and again in his career. Unperturbed, he played brilliantly in his tryouts and made the team, on the way to having a successful season. Looking to transfer to a Division 1 school for his final year of college eligibility, Starks generated plenty of interest but precious few takers. Finally, the coach at Oklahoma State College offered him a scholarship for his senior year. Starks was thrilled. "I went to his office and thanked him, and I told him that I wouldn't let him down," he says. "I played really well that year and we had a winning season. I didn't let him down."

Starks's next hurdle: interesting a professional team in the NBA draft. He wasn't an established college star, and he didn't have the backing of a big-time college coach who would lobby on his behalf. But still he felt that he had a chance to get picked by some NBA team. "I was measuring myself against all these other players who would be drafted, and that's why I felt like I had a shot. Guys like Mitch Richmond and Mookie Blaylock, who are now in the NBA. I had played against them and I really didn't think that they were that far ahead of me." Starks even heard whispers that one NBA coach would take him in the second of the draft's two rounds.

Starks settled in to watch the draft on TV with his wife, Jacqueline, whom he had married while he was at Oklahoma Junior College. One by one, players he knew or had played against got picked by NBA teams, their dreams realized right there on national TV, their smiles as wide as city blocks on the way to the podium. He watched quietly as the second round rolled around, his body tensing with each selection. With only a handful of picks remaining, he held his breath and waited to hear the name "John Starks."

But the name "John Starks" was never called that day.

● ● ●

"I felt bad when it was over," he admits. "I was sitting there praying I'd get drafted, and when I didn't, I felt pretty bad. But at the same time I understood how it worked, and so it wasn't really a devastating blow. I just figured I'd catch on somehow, somewhere."

He was 21 years old and temporarily out of luck. But he wasn't out of reasons to believe in himself. In fact, the thought that he might have aimed too high never once entered his head. As luck would have it, a Starks fan by the name of Larry Brown got the head coaching job with the San Antonio Spurs, and brought

Starks in for a preseason tryout in 1988. This time, when Starks walked into the gym, he saw only 18 or 20 players milling about. The odds were getting better, but they still weren't all that great. He played his heart out in the tryouts, and led the Spurs to an unprecedented win in a preseason tournament as the team's starting point guard. Perhaps his moment had finally arrived, Starks dared to think.

But the Spurs did not guarantee him a job with the club, and once again he was out in the cold, trying to find a spot. Just before the 1988 season began, Golden State Warriors coach Don Nelson summoned Starks to try out for the team. This time, he only had to beat out one player to make the team. Unfortunately, that player was the popular Keith Smart, who had led Indiana University to a college championship the previous year. "Yeah, that was just my luck, to have to beat out Keith Smart," Starks says. "But Coach Nelson gave me a really great shot, and he liked what he saw."

At the end of preseason, Nelson called Starks into his office. "Well, we're going to keep you here, John," Nelson nonchalantly said. "We're going to sign you for the league minimum salary." Starks wasn't listening when Nelson mentioned the salary. He was still stuck on "we're going to keep you here." The dream born on a dirt-floor court and battered by setbacks in high school and college had, in this dingy coach's office, finally come true. "Man, it felt really, really good to hear those words," says Starks. "That was a joyous day for me. So few guys get to the NBA, and considering where I came from, not many people gave me a chance to do it. So it was a great moment to realize that I had finally made it."

The elation would soon wear off. Starks received limited playing time that first year, and got cut right after the season ended.

Not surprisingly, he chose to view his firing in a positive light. "I just chalked it up as a learning experience," he explains. "In my head, I treated that first season as basically my senior year in college. I learned a lot about the NBA, I got the chance to pay against some great players. I never got too down about it. I just looked at where I came from, and I looked at the guys I was competing against and holding my own against. I knew in my heart that I could play at that level. I knew that I belonged." Starks's choppy college career had prepared him for the ups and downs of life in the NBA. By then, he knew enough not to crumble in the face of adversity. He knew that every setback was simply a chance to improve and impress someone else.

That unshakable resolve came in handy when Starks tore up his ankle in an exhibition game before the 1989 season. Forced to miss most of training camp, he was not picked up by any NBA team. As quickly as his dream had come true, now it had fallen apart.

Starks had no choice but to play in the Continental Basketball Association, an NBA outpost for raw college graduates, stubborn aging veterans, and underachieving players of all stripes. Occasionally, someone from the league would make it back to the NBA, but for the most part the CBA was where careers came to die. Players rode in beat-up buses to play in small arenas in front of sparse crowds for even sparser paychecks. It was basketball purgatory, a potential end of the line for lesser talents, a place where resentment and bitterness can really fester—except, that is, to John Starks. "I just looked at the CBA as a stepping stone to where I wanted to go," he says. "It was just another chapter in my life."

Starks played for the Cedar Rapids Silver Bullets, the only

CBA team with its own private jet for players. "That allowed me to pretend that I was still in the NBA," he says. "It helped me keep my spirits up." Still, he adds, "I never, ever forgot where I really was. My goal was to get back to the NBA, and I worked hard to accomplish that every day." Starks won a place on the CBA All-Star team and, in 1990, earned a tryout with one of the NBA's most storied franchises—the New York Knicks.

Few players get even one chance to make it to the big show, and here was Starks with his *second* chance to catch on. Once again, he gave it his all in preseason, but toward the end of camp he sensed that something bad was about to happen. "I just got this feeling that I was about to get cut," he says. "It was the very last day of preseason, and I was having a good practice, but I just had the feeling that this was it for me. I was waiting for someone to come up from behind me and break the bad news."

Perhaps that someone was already on his way to find Starks and cut him loose. But then Starks got lucky—in a way. As the last practice wound down, he drove hard toward the basket, as if one final dunk might affect his fate. He tried to slam the ball over the Knicks star center Patrick Ewing, who must have bristled at the moxie of this little guy taking him on. "Well, Patrick blocked my shot and he also twisted my knee when we hit. I fell down and I thought I had really torn it up. It turned out that it wasn't a major injury, but they still had to put me on the injured reserve list. And they can't cut you from the team if you're on that list. So that was kind of a blessing for me."

Lord knows, John Starks had earned a little good luck. That sprained right knee helped him stay with the New York Knicks in 1990, though he only played sporadically that year. But then, in his second season, the Knicks hired Pat Riley to coach the team.

Riley was the urbane and highly respected coach who had led the Los Angeles Lakers to four world championships in the 1980s. A master motivator, Riley adopted Starks as his star pupil, seeing in him the hidden heart of a champion. "He believed in me from day one," says Starks, with obvious fondness for his former mentor. "He liked the way I played, the passion I brought to the game. Coach Riley taught me a lot about being mentally focused and controlling my emotions. He taught me how to really play the game."

Under Riley, Starks flourished. His minutes—and his points per game—soared. In his first season with the Knicks, he scored fewer than eight points a game. But his average rose to 13.9 in his second season, 17.5 in his third, and 19.0 by the end of 1994. That year, Starks was selected to be on the NBA All-Star team. "I heard that I had been chosen from some reporters," he recalls. "It was an incredible moment. I felt elated. I had not only made it back to the NBA, but now I was an All-Star. Looking at where I came from, that was really something."

Only one more thing and his dream would be complete—an NBA championship ring. In 1994 he helped the Knicks battle their way into the Finals against the Houston Rockets, a powerful team led by superstar Hakeem Olijawon. The scrappy, undrafted grocery bagger from Tulsa was suddenly on a global stage, playing for all the marbles. He proved more than ready for the challenge, averaging nearly 18 points a game in the series against Houston. With the Knicks up three games to two, Starks was simply heroic in the pivotal Game 6, single handedly keeping his team in the game with a series of brilliant shots. Fittingly, he wound up with the ball in his hands as the clock ticked down to nothing. He rose to take a three-point shot from the left side of the court. Hit it, and the Knicks would be world champions. Miss it, and a difficult Game 7 loomed.

Far from being nervous or hesitant, Starks relished the opportunity to win or lose the game. The struggles he had endured to get to this point had steeled him against the effects of pressure, had turned him into a fearless and gutsy warrior. Starks squared up to the basket, jumped high in the air, and launched the shot softly from his fingertips, just as he had a million times before in countless gyms. "That shot was money," Starks recalls. "It felt great when I let it go. I mean, I was in the zone that fourth quarter, and I wanted to be the one to take that shot. I knew that I could make it, and I was happy it was me taking it. And as soon as I released, I thought that it was good."

Perhaps it would have been good, if it had made it. Perhaps it would have swished through the net, giving the Knicks their first championship since 1973. Perhaps then Starks would have been mobbed by his teammates, carried triumphantly off the court atop the shoulders of giants, lauded for the rest of his life as a basketball hero. It certainly would have been a storybook ending to Stark's trying journey.

But Hakeem Olijawon blocked the shot. "He got a fingernail on it," says Starks. "If he hadn't got to it, we would have been walking off that court as champions. I don't think any other center in the league could have blocked that shot. He was very quick and very tall." The ball, barely deflected, sailed harmlessly toward the basket and fell several feet short and wide, ending the game— and, it turned out, the Knicks' chances to win the title. In Game 7, Starks, determined to redeem himself, put on one of the worst displays of shooting in Finals history. He took 18 shots and hit only two, the terrible futility of his performance etched movingly on his face as the game ticked toward its sad conclusion—a Houston victory and the championship. The image of a frustrated Starks nearly crying on the court that night remains one of the most human sports moments of the last decade or so. "I just put too much pressure on myself," he says. "I wanted it so badly, and I just got myself too worked up."

It was the biggest game of his life, and Starks had failed spectacularly.

•••

Few people have ever experienced such brutal defeat on such a visible stage. After the debacle, Starks, his shoulders slumped, trudged miserably off the court and toward the locker room. On the way, Coach Pat Riley grabbed him and gave him some encouragement. "He told me he was proud of me," Starks says. "He said he had lived and died with me all year long, and that he would do it again. That made me feel good, or at least a little better."

After the excruciating Game 7 loss, Starks returned to Tulsa, where the mayor declared an official John Starks Day on June 12, 1994. A good crowd gathered in downtown Tulsa to cheer their native son, and Starks climbed on stage to bask in the kind of glory not many figured he'd ever enjoy. It almost didn't matter that he had come up short in his quest for a title—the important thing was that he ever got the chance to try. "I told the crowd that I was proud of where I had come from. And I talked about the importance of holding on to your dream. All the trials and tribulations that I had to go through to get to this point, and now here I was, I had made it. And I said, 'Don't ever, ever give up on something that you believe in with your heart.' "

Starks never gave up, not even after the stunning failure of Game 7. He went on to become the Knicks' all-time leader in three-point field goals, with nearly 900 made. In 1996, when he lost his starting job and was relegated to the bench, he responded by becoming the very best substitute he could be. For his troubles, he won the NBA's prestigious Sixth Man Award in 1997. After all he had been through, a simple benching wasn't about to dim the fire that burns within John Starks.

Looking back on his long and bumpy road to the NBA, Starks can summon the difficult times only in the context of the glory they helped create. "Honestly, I wouldn't trade the struggles I went through for anything," he says. "They made me a very humble person, and they made me a better man." His belief in God, Starks says, was the reason he was able to persevere. "I always kept my eyes focused on Him, and I always prayed for His help in succeeding. And what He did was put it in my heart that I would never give up, no matter what. A person who lies down is going to have a lot of trouble getting off the ground. And so I'm always standing, always going forward. In my mind I am always fighting to become a better man."

The values that sustained him as he went on his wild and wonderful ride are the values he is now passing on to his eldest son, John Jr. (he has two children and a third on the way). Father and son like to take to the basketball court together, with Starks tutoring his growing teenager in the finer points of the sweet game they both love. Starks didn't have a father to pass him the ball and teach him how to shoot, and he is determined to be the kind of role model he wished he had. Already his son has the same zest and passion for the sport, if not the same tireless work habits. "He thinks I'm a little hard on him, but I tell him it's for his own good," says Starks with a laugh. "But he's got a pretty good feel for the game."

Starks pauses, envisioning his handsome son hoisting shots at a regulation basket—not a rusty tire iron rim like the one he used to aim at. He has traveled far, Starks has, and he feels blessed when he thinks of his son playing ball. "You know, I look at John and I see myself in him," he finally says. "He's going to be taller than I was, but I look at him and I see a little bit of me."

And a little bit, John Starks knows, can go a long, long way.

TIPS FOR TOUGH TIMES

The John Starks Story

*It is defeat that turns bone to flint, and gristle to
muscle, and makes a man invincible.*

Henry Ward Beecher

omeone forget to tell John Starks that guys like him
aren't supposed to become All-Stars in the NBA. Or
maybe it was Starks who forgot to listen. In any case,
*he carved an illustrious and memorable career out of sheer
determination and pluck. All of his setbacks and defeats
forged him into the fearless player who Pat Riley called a
warrior.*

*No, he never won a championship, and, no, he will
never be remembered among the NBA's elite. But he exem-
plifies better than anyone the extraordinary power of perseverance. Every time he faced long odds, Starks dug down a
little deeper and showed he had what it takes. Even when
he was bagging groceries in a Safeway supermarket, he knew
in his heart that he belonged in the NBA. He had many
opportunities to abandon his dream; instead he viewed every
failure as a chance to prove a few more people wrong. If it's
true that winning or losing is secondary to how you play the
game, then John Starks is as great a champion as his sport has
ever seen.*

1. **Make Sure That What You Want, You Want More Than Anything** Only passion can sustain you through the arduous journey toward your goal. Bumps and bruises become badges of honor, as long as you are chasing what is truly in your heart. John Starks knew from the moment he first dunked a basketball that the sport was his only calling, that the NBA was his Holy Grail. That love ensured he would always find the necessary resolve to overcome any obstacles. *Go after the thing that stirs your heart, and you will be able to summon the strength to deal with adversity.*

2. **Don't Let Disappointments Be More Crushing Than They Are** Starks faced a number of setbacks that might have grounded a less determined man. He didn't receive any scholarships during his first 2 years of college; he failed to get drafted by any NBA team; he got cut by the first club that gave him a chance. Any one of those "failures" might have undercut his confidence, allowing fear and doubt to seep into his psyche. But Starks deliberately underplayed the consequences of his setbacks. Banished to the CBA, he became an All-Star in the league and paved the way for his comeback to the NBA. *Dreams aren't soda cans—they shouldn't crush easily.*

3. **Never Stop Believing in Yourself** Others may lose faith in you, but you don't have to jump on the bandwagon. Starks had his share of detractors in the league—people who

felt his cockiness far outdistanced his talent; people who felt he shot too much for someone with such an erratic touch. But Starks had come too far to worry about what anyone thought. He knew what it meant to even have the chance to play, and he was going to make the most of it. Even after shooting a miserable 2 for 18 in Game 7 of the 1994 Finals—a colossal failure that might have permanently crippled his confidence—Starks bounced back to be named the NBA's best sixth man in 1997. *Failure isn't missing a few shots; failure is allowing self-doubt to stop you from taking those shots.*

10 TERMS OF ENCHANTMENT

The Denice Frankhart Story

When you're challenged, it gives you the chance to use more of your brain. It gives you the chance to truly discover yourself.

Denice Frankhart

The first time Denice Frankhart died was on a quarter-mile asphalt racetrack. She was a member of a racecar's pit crew, and she had been sitting on the tailgate of a pickup truck going 40 miles per hour. The truck was on its way to fetch the racecar, which had just finished its trip down the track. Halfway there, for some mysterious reason, Frankhart tumbled off the truck. "Some people say it hit a bump and I lost my balance," she says. "But I had ridden on that truck at races all over the west coast. So I just don't buy that."

Whatever the reason for the fall, it was devastating. Frankhart landed standing up, and the soles of her tennis sneakers were torn off. Her left ankle twisted all the way around, totally destroying it. She broke her chest, and cracked most of her teeth as well. The skin on both of her elbows was completely shredded. Worst of all, she banged the back of her head on the track, fracturing her skull and damaging her brain stem. "I have no memory of it at all," she says. "The last thing I remember is hopping up on to that truck." By the time paramedics reached her, her heart had stopped beating. Clinically, Denice Frankhart was dead.

A doctor at the track revived her, but she died again in the ambulance. Then she died a third time at the hospital. She spent the next 6¹/₂ weeks in a coma. In that time, all her friends abandoned her, and all her hopes for a future were dashed. She woke up unable to walk, speak, read, or do much of anything. The accident had completely shattered her life.

It was the very best thing that ever happened to her.

• • •

Adversity was nothing new to Frankhart; in fact, she was born to it. She grew up in a dysfunctional home in southern California, with a philandering father who neglected his family and a mother who leaned too heavily on her eight children. "My father had other girlfriends and other children on the side," remembers Frankhart. "And so we were the last ones to get his time or his money." Without income from her husband, Frankhart's mother did her best to put food on the table, working as a motel maid for $1.65 an hour. Emotionally, though, she didn't have much to offer. "Basically, she turned to me for support because I was the strongest child," says Frankhart. "It was almost like I was the mother and she was the child."

Frankhart learned to be resourceful from an early age. To help in the kitchen, young Denice would catch crayfish at a trout farm by using a willow branch with bubblegum stuck to the end. Once she'd caught 25 crayfish and put them in her empty coffee can, she'd run home so they could be cooked for dinner. For entertainment, she and her siblings were forced to be inventive, and so they invented their very own swimming pool. They would go over to Knott's Berry Farm across the street and steal a huge crate that was slated to be crushed. "Then we'd get some heavy-duty plastic that my father used in his construction business, and we'd line the inside of the crate in plastic," Frankhart says. "We'd clip on the plastic with clothespins, fill it up with water from a hose and jump right in. Pretty soon all the kids from the neighborhood were coming over to swim in our pool." When enough kids got in, their makeshift pool would collapse. Frankhart would simply go get another crate and start all over again.

By the time she was 8 years old, Frankhart had to start earning money to help her family. Her first job was pulling weeds for 25 cents an hour. From there, she graduated to cleaning people's homes. By far her most memorable job had to do with a next-door neighbor who needed a special service. "She was this really obese woman, and when she drove home after work, she would pay us a nickel to help pull her out of her car," Frankhart says. "But what she didn't know was that some of us were selling tickets to other kids to come over and look over our fence and watch this obese woman swim in her pool."

Frankhart showed an ability to handle responsibility beyond her years. When she was 10, she babysat children who were only a few years younger than she was. At 12 she was hired to take care of a 4-year-old boy while the boy's mother worked at Disneyland. "Every Saturday and Sunday I would take the boy to Disneyland and spend all day riding the rides for free. That was maybe the best job I ever had." After that she worked two jobs while going to school in between: she would rise at 3:30 a.m. to bake pies and biscuits at a nearby motel restaurant, and then, in the evening, go to work at a medieval-themed restaurant, where she served as a waitress, hostess, and even part-time accountant. Her coworkers were convinced she was 22 years old. She was really 16.

In this way did Denice Frankhart sacrifice most of her child-hood. "To me it seems like I never really got the chance to be a kid," she says. Whenever he was around, her father would make her drive to the store in his car to fetch supplies for him. The first time she did it, she was 13. "Three years later I bought a neigh-bor's station wagon for myself," she says. "I paid him $300 and spent the next year paying off the rest." But as mature as she seemed, Frankhart was actually suffering from a lack of love and attention. "I think the only present I got in my whole life was this huge doll my father got me this one time," she says. "Well, I was so mad at him, so mad at the way he treated us, why the heck would I want his stupid doll? I remember I ripped the foot off the doll right in front of him." Frankhart hated her father so much that, late one night, she snuck into his closet, came out with one of his hunting rifles, woke him up by cocking it, and told him she would shoot him dead if he so much as moved a muscle. "After I told him that," she says, "the next thing I said was, 'Please move a muscle.'"

It was a life filled with pain and sadness, insults and humilia-tion. After her parents divorced at last, her father would raid the house and steal as much as he could, as a way to get back at his ex-wife. All he was really doing was harming his own children. Finally, says Frankhart, her father tried to burn their house down. "He was just this mean, sadistic person," she says. "I could not wait to get away from him."

She managed that by getting married when she turned 18. "Like my father, he was an alcoholic, but at least he wasn't mean to me," she says. "Still, he would drink every day after work, and after a while I just couldn't take it." Frankhart would get dinner ready for two every evening, knowing full well her husband would not join her. "I was so unhappy that all I did was eat. I would eat a whole gallon of ice cream, anything I could find that was fattening. I used to think that it was because as a kid we never had much food. But what I think I was really doing was making myself really fat because of my husband. I wanted to make myself look ugly because he didn't deserve me. Why should I make myself look good for him?" She entered the marriage weighing 175 pounds; she left it 5 years later weighing 225.

But Frankhart was determined to pull herself together. She rented a pretty townhouse with two friends, and started running every day to get herself in shape. She worked for a medical company, learning as she went. "I took x-rays, did office stuff, whatever was needed," she says. "I didn't have a license for anything, but I knew how to do everything." On the surface things looked like they were finally going Frankhart's way, but in fact she had once again put herself in a tricky situation. One roommate got pregnant with a 15–year-old boy; the other became a heroin addict. "And both of them were hanging on me for support, just like my mom used to. I was the one who could handle the most responsibility, and so they would look to me to be strong. After a while of that I just couldn't breathe."

From that fire, Frankhart jumped into another frying pan. She began an affair with a married man, knowing full well the relationship had no future. "I told myself I didn't want to get married again, and that this affair was safe for me," she explains. "He lived with me 3 days a week, and the other 4 with his wife. But I was not in love with this man. It was just something to help me get by." The man drove a funny car in a racing circuit all over California, and so Frankhart learned all she could about automobiles, as a way to make herself useful and tag along. She did, indeed, become a valuable member of the pit crew, pitching in under the hood, helping out in the office, washing and waxing the car—doing whatever was needed. Once again, on the surface, it looked like a reasonably stable life. But, deep down, Frankhart was as miserable as ever. "I wasn't happy with the way my life was going," she says. "For a long, long time I was totally lost. I didn't know what I was going to do, how I was going to end up. I felt that I had really failed to live my life the right way."

She might have gone on like that, a failure inside, for years, even decades. The failure that she felt was something she could suppress, just like she had buried so many bad feelings before. She didn't even know exactly how bad her life had become because that kind of adversity was all she'd ever known. Quite simply, she did not respect herself, and so no one respected her. She wasn't getting much out of life because she wasn't asking for much. She was smart, resourceful, strong, and good, but inside she felt worthless. Never allowed to act like a child when she was young, she had chosen to act like one now.

•••

All that changed on a warm September night in 1980, at the Speed Drum racetrack in Las Vegas. Frankhart was working as part of the pit crew for her boyfriend's racecar, something "not many women did at that time," she says. "We would drive over after the race, pull the driver out, check the batteries, roll up the car's parachute, back it into the truck, all that kind of stuff. I had learned a lot about cars and I really knew what I was doing." She hopped onto the truck's tailgate, the way she always did. Not once before had she so much as slipped, much less lost her grip. But this time, halfway down the quarter-mile track, something caused

Frankhart to fall. To this day she does not know exactly what happened, only that she woke up several weeks later in Las Vegas's Mercy Hospital. In a wildly figurative sense, the fall might have represented her lack of grounding in real life. Completely lost, with nothing to hold on to, Frankhart had fallen long before she tumbled off that truck.

And as dark as her life had been up to that point, it was about to get darker. Revived a third time, she spent 6½ weeks in a coma. Later she was told that when people came to the hospital to see her, she would try to bite their hands. "Don't get too close," guests were told, "Denice bites." Frankhart believes she was merely reacting to the mistreatment she says she suffered at the hands of hospital nurses. "Let me tell you, when you're in a coma, you can sense what's going on. And that's why, when people come out of comas, they are often really angry. It's because they want to kill the first person they see. I had a lot of anger inside once I woke up. I threw a mean bedpan."

Frankhart could not walk or speak or even read. Doctors told her she narrowly missed becoming a quadriplegic. As it was, she would have to learn how to walk and talk all over again. Early on, her friends and family came to visit her in the hospital, but after a while the visits stopped. "When you're running around with a bad crowd of people, and suddenly you have nothing to offer them, they disappear really fast," she says. One night she sat up in her hospital bed and felt a terrifying sense of dread. "I realized that I was all alone in this world," she says. "I felt completely empty inside. I didn't know where I would go from there, I didn't know what would happen to me. It was just this awful, hopeless feeling." Frankhart even wondered why it was that she had survived.

She turned to God for the answer, seeking his counsel late one night. He did not appear in the flesh, or even speak to her directly. But she felt an odd presence in her lonely hospital room. "I was asking, 'What's going on, why is this happening to me?' " she recalls. "And then, all of a sudden, all the events of my life started unfolding in my mind. All the good things and all the bad things, from the moment I was born right up to that point. And I felt happy and sad and every emotion you could possibly feel. And I guess I realized that it didn't have to be the way it was."

Frankhart finally left the hospital and returned to her home in California. Unable to work, she was forced to go on welfare. Eventually, an insurance settlement took care of her financially, but physically the road back to health would be a bumpy one. A full year passed before she was able to utter a complete sentence. For months she could not crawl across the floor, much less walk across a room. "My physical therapists came over every day, and they would wrap a belt around my waist as I lay on the floor. And then they would pull on this belt until I could get myself up into a kneeling position. I was literally learning how to crawl all over again."

And yet, despite her dire situation, something was different. After she returned from the hospital, her mother came to live with her in her home. Before too long, Frankhart felt like a child once more. "She was doing it again, leaning on me, sucking the life out of me," says Frankhart. "Here I was, I couldn't talk, I couldn't walk, I had brain damage, I was really hurt. And it seemed to me like she couldn't care less." Then Frankhart did something she might not have been able to do before the accident: 2 months into her mother's stay, Frankhart kicked her out.

It was one of the very first times in her life she had asserted herself. The bottom line was that she needed all her energy to get better. The turning point came when she finally rose out of her wheelchair and took three tiny steps. "I was standing about 5 feet away from the fireplace," she says. "My therapists were standing next to me, and when I got up my body was shaking like crazy. And they helped me get my balance, but then they kept trying to let me go, to keep me from grabbing on. The only way to learn to walk on your own is to let go."

So Frankhart let go, and somehow managed to stay on her feet. Then she slowly took three unsteady steps toward the fireplace. "That was maybe the greatest day of my whole life because it was the first day that I felt like I had hope," she says. "Before that I had a real fear that I would never get out of my wheelchair. But that day I realized that my two feet would be like anchors to me. I realized that there was a future for me."

The next important event occurred the day that Frankhart went to her savings and loan to do some banking. By then, she was relying on a cane, sometimes staggering and sometimes shuffling, but walking nonetheless. Her speech was a little slurry, and her manner a little slow, but it was important for her to do as much as she could for herself. And so she approached the teller's window, determined to conduct her business like any other customer.

The teller took one look at her and instantly sized her up. "He started speaking very loudly, exaggerating everything he said, treating me like a child," says Frankhart. "It was just a rude, lousy way to treat a customer. And for some reason I thought of all the bad things I had put up with in my life. And so I stood there and said to myself, 'Okay, enough is enough.' "

What she said to the teller was a little more direct. "I may be disabled," she advised him, "but I'm not an idiot." She never once raised her voice, but she did deploy a withering look. The teller did not utter another word. "I also told him that my money is as good as anyone else's," Frankhart says. "And that if he couldn't show me respect, I would take my business to someone who could." With that, the other customers in the bank broke into applause.

It was a monumental moment in her life. "I knew right then that it was the beginning of my future," she says. "It was the day that I realized how people with disabilities are viewed. They are often looked at as less than a whole person. And I was not going to put up with that kind of discrimination." Frankhart decided to rally others to her cause, and made it her mission to help disabled people stand up for themselves. Her first stop was the Melody Land Christian Center, a home for people who were mentally challenged. "I called the nuns and I asked if I could come over and speak with these people. They said sure, and so I talked to them about how blessed they all are. I told them they were lucky to have people fixing their meals and taking care of their medication. I told them at least they didn't have to put up with people calling all day to try and give them credit cards. My point was that they should start thinking of themselves as special and blessed."

Right away, Frankhart could tell that her message was getting through. "Then she started going around to homeless people and handing them little cards to cheer them up," says Frankhart's friend Robbie Motter, president of the Professional Women's Roundtable, an organization that support's women's businesses in Riverside, California. "She had these cards in her glove compartment, and when she saw someone she'd just give them a little card with a positive message on it. And I'm sure that whoever got these cards, it really made their day. Who knows how many peoples' lives she might have turned around that way?"

Nursing homes, convalescent hospitals, rehab centers, local schools—Frankhart gave inspirational speeches to any group that would have her. Her message was always the same—believe in yourself, and don't ever let anyone or anything shake that belief. "When you are disabled, or when you face some other challenge, it's like you have to learn to do something a brand new way. And so it's more of an opportunity than it is a setback. When you're challenged, it gives you the chance to use more of your brain. It gives you the chance to truly discover yourself."

Frankhart's message inspired countless people, but the biggest beneficiary was herself. "For the first time in my life, I felt really fulfilled," she says, fighting back tears. "I just felt so damn good about myself. When I was a kid I was always fat or stupid or something else negative. But now I was doing something that I was meant to do. For the first time I was living my life the way I wanted to." Looking back on the day she fell off a pickup truck, Frankhart makes a startling admission. "If somehow I went back to before the accident happened, I would be the first one on line to have it happen to me again," she says. "Because I am such a better person now than I was before. I appreciate all the good things in life, and I don't let any of the little things get me down. I am just a stronger, better person, and I don't let anyone take advantage of me anymore."

●●●

As soon as she stopped allowing herself to be treated as if she were undeserving, Denice Frankhart saw her luck start to change.

After returning to the hospital with complications in 1985, she met a nurse-in-training who helped get her back on her feet. "He helped me walk, he helped me talk, he took me out, and wasn't embarrassed to be seen with me," she says. "He was the first man in my life who didn't make me feel small." Frankhart got married in a $25 white lace dress, with her mother-in-law as her maid of honor. Fifteen friends each brought a dish, and the justice of the peace looked exactly like Colonel Sanders. "We just had the best time that day," she says. "For the first time in my life I had a stable family life. And now it's 15 years later and I am still on cloud nine."

Frankhart had one other unfulfilled dream—to travel the world. She liked to leaf through the travel section in the Sunday paper, just to read about faraway places and exotic trips. Then she read about a class for travel agents. She signed up and passed it with flying colors. She got her travel agent's license and decided to specialize in cruises. She spent $50,000 of her insurance settlement to pay for eight cruises, so she would be able to answer any questions her clients had for her. That's when she discovered just how hard traveling can be for people with disabilities. "And not just on the boat itself, but once you reached the destination, too," she says. "Islands with nothing but steep steps, places that just weren't accessible to wheelchairs: there were a lot of reasons to fear traveling." A few agencies offered special trips for disabled people, but none offered what they needed the most—assurance that their needs would be met. "I knew the difficulties of traveling and I knew I had a lot of questions. And I knew that if I had them, a lot of other people must have them too."

And so Enchanted Travel Tours was born. "I picked the name because I want my life to be enchanting," Frankhart says. "A lot of people who are disabled accept whatever they can get, when what they should be doing is trying to make some magic." Frankhart opened her agency in Riverside, California, and spent 3 years researching different cruise ships and ports of call. She came up with innovations such as rounding up her client's medical records and sharing them with the cruise ship's doctors. "She took it one step further than other agencies," says her friend Robbie Motter. "If a cruise company says, 'Oh yeah, we take care of the handicapped,' Denice is going to get on board and check it out herself. Is this aisle wide enough for a wheelchair? Have you considered that blind people have dogs? Denice went the extra mile, but only because she has faced some of those things and understands the importance of taking care of them."

Now, Enchanted Travel Tours is a smashing success. Frankhart gets lots of letters from happy customers, as well as e-mails from all over the world, asking for her help in establishing similar agencies. This year, Robbie Motter nominated her for the U.S. Small Business Administration's National Welfare to Work Entrepreneur of the year 2000. Frankhart won the award and was invited to come to the White House, where she met President Clinton. "Her story is an inspiration for everyone," said SBA District Director Sandy Sutton. "She demonstrates that with drive and determination we can overcome any obstacle." Adds Motter, "The thing I admire most about her is her tenacity. She was in a coma, she couldn't walk, she couldn't talk, even her own family couldn't deal with her disability. But she didn't let any of those things stop her." In fact, says Motter, "It took the terrible things that happened to her for her to end up where she is. She never dreamed of going into business, but because of her tragedy she saw a real need, and now she is addressing it."

The little girl who cobbled together her own swimming pool is now a wonderful woman who created a brand new life. She did it by falling as low as she could go, and by fighting through the worst ordeal of her life. She had to reach depths she had never fathomed, and then she had to let go—literally—of her old way of living. It took failure for Frankhart to have a chance to succeed. It took dying for her to have the chance to really live.

"That's the beauty of it," she says. "A lot of times when people are down and out, all they want to do is get back to where they were. But you are really shortchanging yourself if you settle for the status quo. Because the truth is you can have anything you want—all you have to do is ask. And there's no better time to start over then when you're down and out."

TIPS FOR TOUGH TIMES

The Denice Frankhart Story

I have found that failure is really God's way of saying, "Excuse me, you're moving in the wrong direction."

Oprah Winfrey

It's hard to believe that anyone could consider dying a good thing, but Denice Frankhart absolutely does. Had she not fallen off a moving pickup truck and clinically died three times before being revived, she would not have found the strength to become who she is today. It took a jarring and nearly fatal accident for Frankhart to realize that her life had spun completely out of control—and that she was capable of changing the way she lived.

Frankhart would not be defined by the fall that left her disabled. Instead, she has been defined by her response to it. Rather than feel victimized—as she had since she was a child—Frankhart found a way to stand up for herself and others like her. She felt like a failure in her life right up to the moment that she almost left it, but after that she challenged herself to be the person she always wanted to be. Most people won't have to hit bottom as dramatically as Frankhart did in order to rediscover themselves, but her experience is a *heightened example of the cleansing and rejuvenating effect adversity can have.*

1. **Respecting Yourself Invites Success** No one will ever take you seriously if you don't take yourself seriously first. Frankhart spent much of her adult life trapped in a web of self-loathing and self-doubt. It was only after she began to respect herself that people treated her with respect. Even though the accident left her physically weaker and more vulnerable than ever, Frankhart emerged from the wreckage with a newfound love for herself—and that made her a stronger, more successful human being. *Don't allow failure and adversity to lessen your self-esteem; respect yourself through thick and thin and others will follow suit.*

2. **Let Go of Old Ways and Bad Habits** It's always easier to do nothing than to change the things that need to be changed. But sometimes letting go of your old way of living is the most important thing that you can do. Frankhart stumbled her way through life allowing others to take advantage of her. But that all stopped when she lapsed into a coma, and awakened with the chance to change her life. The day she let go of her physical therapists and took three steps on her own was the day she literally let go of her old lifestyle. *Force yourself to relinquish habits and traits that lead to failure—the crutches that make you feel secure but actually keep you unfulfilled.*

3. **Don't Settle for the Status Quo**   Seize upon the opportunity that failure presents to redefine yourself and your goals. Don't simply try and get back to where you were; aim much higher. In Frankhart's case, recapturing her old lifestyle was hardly a worthy goal, and she wisely refused to shortchange herself that way. The pain and hardship she endured fundamentally changed her, and in that way failure can be considered a rebirth. *Square one is the ideal place to launch a dream, so take advantage of the chance to rise beyond expectations.*

11 TAKING STOCK

The Chris Gardner Story

When things are going badly and you really want to quit, that's the time to push harder than ever. The game doesn't start until you're up against the wall.

Chris Gardner

"So what's the big piece?" Chris Gardner is asking. "How big is big?" Gardner sits in his 45th-floor apartment in New York City's swanky Trump Tower, high above Fifth Avenue and overlooking the gorgeous sprawl of Central Park. He leans back in his plush chair, his white dress shirt unbuttoned with no tie or jacket in sight, a telephone pressed between his broad shoulder and shaved head. Jazz music plays in the background, and behind him, propped against a window, is one of the few decorations in the sparsely decorated room—a sign that says, simply, "Imagine." Gardner is relaxed, assured, totally at ease: he handles the business call like he might handle a casual chat about a Knicks game that night or a discussion with a friend about some hot new restaurant. "Okay," he says softly into the phone. "Sweet."

He is talking about a deal worth *billions* of dollars.

When the stakes are high and the payoff huge, Gardner is in his element. "I'm an adrenaline junkie," he explains after hanging up. "I get up for the elephant hunt. Since I've been in the business, I've always had a nose for the big trade. I can hit the singles and doubles, and that's fine. But every time I'm up there I'm swinging for the fences. Every time." The president and CEO of Gardner Rich Co., the successful Chicago-based brokerage house he started in 1989, Gardner may get juiced over big deals, but he demonstrates an uncanny calm and poise while working, sort of like Michael Jordan in the closing seconds of a tight basketball game. Tall and fit at 45, he has a loose and confident style, and a prized symbol of his success is the stunning black Ferrari he purchased from another Chicago entrepreneur who did okay—Michael Jordan himself. Put simply, Gardner is not your typical, button-downed, briefcase carrying Wall Street type: he's more like a happy Zen surfer riding one heck of a wave. "I'm good at this," he says matter-of- factly. "And as far as what I do, how I make my money, how I build my business, there is no one out there on the street who does it the way I do."

That's because there's no one out there quite like Chris Gardner—a man who not that long ago was a poor and homeless single parent sleeping in a subway station bathroom with his 16-month-old son.

● ● ●

He grew up without a father, in Delphi, Louisiana, but he did not lack for male role models. His mother's brothers were war veterans who bent Chris's ear with tales of travel and adventure. "I remember hearing all these stories about cities all over the world, and I would run and get a globe or a map and try to spot them," says Gardner. "So from very early on I wanted to go places. I was always on the way *somewhere*."

He lied about his age and enrolled in the Navy, intent on discovering the world beyond Louisiana. Instead, he spent most of his 4 years of service as a medic on American bases. He may not have seen the world, but he did discover something inside himself. "I learned what I was capable of, and that was anything I set my mind on," he says. "Those were the best 4 years of my life." Gardner worked with top-notch surgeons and might have even gone to medical school had it not been for his desire to earn money quickly, and not spend years and years in training. And so, after the navy, he took a job selling medical supplies in Silicon Valley, California. He was on a sales call one day, a heavy catalogue and dozens of free samples tucked under his arms, when he met a man who forever changed his life. "He's in this car driving around the parking lot looking for a space, and I wave him over and tell him I'm leaving my spot," Gardner recalls. "This was the sharpest guy I had ever seen in my life. His demeanor, his hair, his suit, the way it fit him. *And* he was driving a gorgeous red Ferrari." Gardner asked the man what he did, and discovered he was a stockbroker who made $80,000 a month. That was all that Chris Gardner needed to hear.

He applied for a training position in the brokerage house Dean Witter, and endured 10 long months of interviews. The problem? "I didn't fit the profile of a stockbroker," he says. "I never went to college, so I had no college buddies I could network with. I wasn't from a politically connected family, and I didn't have my own money. What, then, was my connection to money? What was I going to bring to the job?" On top of all that, Gardner was a black man trying to enter a largely white world, and that alone might have dissuaded others from chasing the dream that Gardner chose to pursue. But he was nothing if not driven, and after 10 months he was finally hired at Dean Witter, and told to report to work one Monday morning. "So I go in and the man who hired me had gotten axed over the weekend," he says. "The people were like, 'Who are you? We don't know you.' I had to leave and go home."

The bad luck was only just beginning. When he got home, Gardner saw that his girlfriend had left him and carted away all his possessions, as well as their young son Chris. "She took everything but the dust," says Gardner. Devastated, he sat on his stoop and pondered his loss, until some cops pulled up and ran the license plates on his car, which was double-parked out front. "I had $1200 in unpaid parking tickets," he explains. "And in California, they have a rule: 'You can't pay, you have to stay.' So I went to jail."

They put him in a cell with three other men—a rapist, an arsonist, and a murderer. "Everybody tells their little story of how they got there," says Gardner. "And when they asked me how I got there, I told them, 'Attempted murder, and I will try it again.' " His sentence was 10 days in the slammer, a disaster since on the ninth day he had a scheduled interview at Dean Witter. "I've got this meeting with the big Kahuna and I'm sitting in jail!" he says. "I've got to find a way out of this situation. That's when my focus thing kicked in."

What Gardner calls his "focus thing" is his ability to fixate on a situation until it is under his control. "I am capable of extreme focus," he says. "For very, very long periods of time. Some deals, I work on them for 4 years. People say, 'Why are you sweating that now?' But I know how it works and I know what I have to do. And it requires extreme focus." Sitting in that jail cell, Gardner had to find some way to seize control of his situation, to not let the easy excuse of his incarceration undermine his dream. What he did was persuade a guard to let him make a phone call, so that he could postpone his interview for a couple of days. "It's the same

thing I do today," says Gardner. "It's making your agenda someone else's agenda." What's more, Gardner was showing the people skills he calls one of his greatest strengths. "If I could put relationships on my balance sheet, I'd be the richest man in Wall
Street," he says. "Relationships are 90 percent of the game to me,
and I am very good at them. In this business, it's not just who you
know, it's what will who you know *do* for you?"

Getting the guard to let him make a phone call was proof positive of that maxim. But then, after he was released, Gardner had
another problem: no clean clothes. And so he went on the biggest
interview of his life in the same bell-bottom jeans, maroon jacket,
and beat-up Addidas sneakers he had worn in jail for 10 days. "I
couldn't think of a lie bizarre enough to tell this guy, so I told him
the truth," remembers Gardner. "Turns out he had been divorced
four times, so he spent the whole interview telling me stories
about his wives." The next day, Gardner got a phone call at the
home of a friend where he was staying. He got the job.

Things were looking up, but the odds were still against him.
Yes, Gardner now had a good job, and he was able to move into
a boarding house while he studied for his stockbroker's exam. But
the exam was a brutal 8-hour ordeal, with a failure rate of 70 percent. Gardner worked long hours at the firm, then went home
and boned up on equities, municipals, and convertible bonds.
Some nights he even slept under his desk at Dean Witter.
"Nobody knew," he says. "I'd be up before anyone arrived, freshen
up as best I could, and knock off 20 calls while the other trainees
were sitting drinking their coffee and reading their papers." Every
minute of Gardner's day was dedicated to fulfilling his dream, to
digging his way up from the bottom. He had no time for distrac-
tions of any kind.

Then, one day, the doorbell rang. It was his ex-girlfriend, returning something she had taken: Gardner's 1-year-old son, Chris.

Gardner knew one thing: he would keep the boy and be the father he never had. An instant single parent, he got kicked out of the boarding house, which did not take children. He and his son lived for a while in a cheap motel, but eventually moved into the first homeless shelter established in San Francisco. "The rules were simple," says Gardner. "It was a place to sleep, not a place to live. You must be out by 8:00 a.m., and you have to either be working or looking for work. You have no key to your room, and if you leave anything in it, it will not be there when you come back. You never get the same room twice, and when you come back at night they'll only give you a room if one is available. I did that for 3 months, me and the baby."

Every morning, Gardner would have to pack up all his worldly possessions. "I had the baby in his stroller, my briefcase, the biggest bag of Pampers in the world, a duffel bag with all his clothes in it, and two suits—the one on my back and one in a hanging bag. And an umbrella. And that was it." Some nights, however, there were no rooms available when Gardner and his son, retrieved from a day-care center, returned to the shelter at night. On those nights, he took young Chris to the Macarthur Station of the Bay Area Rapid Transit system in San Francisco, a sprawling train depot with a bathroom that locked from the inside. "It was a big and clean bathroom," says Gardner. "So we would go in there and lock the door and take a nap, spend a few hours, freshen up, whatever. I had to coach my boy to play this little game: when people banged on the door we were both as quiet as we could be. But the station was big enough that when people couldn't get in, they just left and looked for another john."

Money was tight for Gardner, who had yet to pass his stock-broker's exam and start earning a broker's salary. "Where we lived there were these prostitutes who used to give my son $5 here and there because he was so cute," says Gardner. "The truth is, if it weren't for those ladies, there were days when I might not have been able to feed my boy." His money woes made it harder for him to stay focused on his goal. They even made him wonder if his course of action had been wise. Here he was, barely able to feed himself and his son. Why in the world did he think that he could ever be a stockbroker?

• • •

Somehow, Gardner held fast to his dream, and passed his stockbroker's exam with flying colors. He went to work at Dean Witter, and after a year was recruited by a rival brokerage, Bear Stearns. He was told that he was just what they were looking for—a PSD. "Poor, smart, and driven," says Gardner. "People with a deep desire to get ahead. Those were the kinds of people they were looking for, and those are still the kinds of people I like to surround myself with." Gardner now had his foot in the door at Bear Stearns, but he would have a tougher go of it than the other stock-brokers. "At the time there were very few blacks in the firm or even in the industry," says Bob Muh, then a senior managing director at Bear Stearns and now the CEO of Sutter Securities in San Francisco. "It was a disadvantage, but Chris found a way to make it an advantage. He knew everyone was evaluating him, and he was incredibly professional in everything he did. I have rarely met anyone who was as driven and motivated as Chris." One of the keys to Gardner's success was "that he was never afraid to ask about something if he didn't know the answer," says Muh. "He wasn't embarrassed to ask for help, and to this day, he'll call once in a while to discuss something. He was one of the best askers around, and one of the best listeners." Passing the exam was one thing, but becoming a good stockbroker is a difficult and lengthy process, and Muh was most impressed by Gardner's perseverance. "It didn't happen overnight, and there was a lot of frustration along the way," says Muh. "But Chris was hungry. He never forgot where he came from, and he never took his eye off the ball."

Gardner eventually earned as much as $300,000 a year at Bear Stearns, but the big-game hunter in him could not be suppressed. In 1989 he started his own brokerage house out of his Chicago apartment, with a whopping bankroll of $10,000. It was a risky move, considering he had limited capital and no backing behind him. But it was then that the experience of his setbacks and failures proved most useful. "Being homeless and starting a business from scratch are very similar endeavors," says Gardner. "You have a lack of resources, and you have to make something out of nothing. The skills I learned being homeless were *exactly* transferable to starting Gardner Rich. Today, young people always ask me what they should be doing to get ready for their careers. And I always say, 'Try being homeless.' They don't want to hear that, but my point in saying it is that the best training is making something out of nothing, with no one around to bail you out."

Last year, Gardner's company did some $10 million in business, and this year is on track to do much, much more. He is working a couple of major deals, including the billion-dollar elephant he hopes to bag sometime soon (his cut would be in the millions). He is also a big-time philanthropist, donating $500,000 to educational causes over the past 4 years. In 1990 he produced a motivational booklet called *Hard Work Pays*, which he distributed to 100,000 seventh graders. On its cover: a picture of the Ferrari Gardner bought from Michael Jordan, whom he met at a Ferrari repair shop. The dazzling black car—which Gardner says "is so sleek it's the car Darth Vadar would drive"—has a license plate that reads "NOT MJ." The message is a simple one. "You don't have to be a dope dealer or a ballplayer to succeed," says Gardner, whose own son Chris is now in college (he also has a teenaged daughter who shows an aptitude for business). "You just have to be smart, and you have to be extremely focused."

Above all else, says Gardner, you have to hang in there in the face of adversity. Sharing a jail cell with hardened criminals and sleeping in a public bathroom were, to be sure, traumatic experiences, and might have been the straws that broke Gardner's back. After all, he wasn't a likely candidate for stockbroker to begin with: the added stress of his personal failings might have been enough crush his fragile dream. But he was determined to be the good father that he wished he had had, and to become the success his uncles inspired him to be. "Up against the wall is not a comfortable place to be, and a lesser person is going to crack and have a convenient excuse for why they got into drugs or alcohol," says Gardner. "But when things are really bad you have to dig the deepest and say, 'How can I get out of here?' Not 'Can I?' But '*How* can I?' When things are going badly and you really want to quit, that's the time to push harder than ever before. The game doesn't start until you're up against the wall."

Of course, it helps to get a little boost along the way. Gardner remembers one particularly trying night when his dreams of success seemed remote indeed. The lights were shut off where he was staying, forcing him to bathe his little son by candlelight. "That was the night when I thought to myself, 'Man, oh man, I'm beat. This is it, you tried your best but it's all over. Might as well hang it up,' " says Gardner.

And then Gardner's beautiful son did something wonderful. "He just looked up at me from the bathtub with his big eyes and said, 'You know what, poppa? You're a good poppa.' " Gardner fights back tears at the memory. "I needed to hear something like that right then. It was as if God had told him to say it."

TIPS FOR TOUGH TIMES

The Chris Gardner Story

*Many of life's failures are people who did not
realize how close they were to success when they
gave up.*

Thomas Edison

hris Gardner could not get further from his dream of
becoming a stockbroker than living in a restroom in a
busy subway station. Or so one might surmise. In fact,
Gardner knew that he was closer than it seemed from
appearances. He simply had to endure the consequences of his
mistakes and stay on his feet; he had to keep going despite
the fact that the trail he was taking had never been blazed
before.

Gardner managed to hold it together in situations that
might have caused others to crack. The calm resourcefulness
he showed when times were tough helped him become the
fearless wheeler-dealer he is today. He had every reason to
give up—and enough excuses to fill a small notebook—but
he knew that keeping himself in the game was more than
half the battle. Quitting on his dream would have ensured
failure; plugging away gave him the chance to ultimately
succeed. Although there were many hardships to distract him,
Gardner never lost sight of his dream—and still hasn't.

1. **Stay Extremely Focused** Gardner has an uncanny ability to concentrate on problems for long periods of time. That intense focus came in particularly handy when Gardner's world crashed down around him. But even if you don't wind up in jail or on the street, focus is the key to keeping your dreams close at hand. Somehow, Gardner managed to study for his stockbroker's exam even while worrying where the next meal for his son would come from. *When failure creates chaos and hardship in your life, that is precisely the time that you must remain extremely focused on your goal.*

2. **Don't Ask "Can I?," Ask "*How* Can I?"** Gardner always displayed remarkable self-confidence, even when he was locked in jail alongside hardened criminals. When it looked like he wouldn't be freed in time to make an important interview, he didn't wonder whether or not he would make it, he simply tried to figure out exactly how he would do it. As Gardner likes to put it, he made his agenda someone else's agenda. Coping with failure is easier when you limit your options to only one—find a way to overcome the obstacle at hand. *Don't waste energy wondering if you can extract yourself from some mess; devote all your energy to figuring out how.*

3. **When You're Up Against the Wall, Push the Wall Down** We will never know how strong we really are unless we are truly

tested. Gardner passed his many tests with flying colors. He was barely managing to support himself and his kid; what made him think he could ever be a bigtime stockbroker? In fact, the skills he drew upon when he was at his lowest were the very skills he used to create his own company. Few of us will ever know what it's like to sleep in a public bathroom, but whatever wall we happen to find ourselves up against, the reaction should be the same—dig down deep and summon the strength to push the wall away. *Failure is a crucible that tests our ultimate resolve, and on the other side of the challenge is the success we seek.*

12 INVINCIBLE SUMMER

The Ben Jones Story

In the midst of winter I discovered there was within me an invincible summer.

Albert Camus

He stands there at the starting line and takes a deep breath, this 40-year-old man who has been to hell and back. He stands there waiting for the starting gun to sound, his body nearly shuddering with anticipation. All he wants to do is run, to feel his legs power him forward, to feel the wind on his face and the air in his lungs and the sweat on his brow. Years earlier he had watched this same race—the Peachtree 10K Run in Atlanta, Georgia—from inside the Stein Club, a dingy bar along Peachtree Street. Back then he would watch the runners gallop past and shake his head and say to himself, "Look at these fools out there, running around for no reason." Back then, his only exercise was bellying up to the bar and lifting a glass of booze to his mouth. "Hell, I couldn't even get up and go to the bathroom without falling down," he recalls. "Physically, mentally, spiritually, I was dead. I was finished."

Standing at the starting line, he thinks how truly strange it is that he is even there. He has spent long nights in jails and in gutters, and he has seen his friends shun him on the street. He has also starred on a top-rated TV series. Many times he has felt like he did not want to live; other times he has gazed out airplane windows and thanked the good Lord for his life on earth. Then he hears the words, "On your mark, get set..." and he slips into a crouch. The gun blasts, and Ben Jones is off and running.

He is not the swiftest runner in the field, not by a long shot. But he is surely the most unlikely contestant in the bunch. Only a few years earlier, Ben Jones was doing all he could to kill himself—and very nearly succeeded one terrifying September night in 1977. "I was dying of alcoholism, which is a chronic, progressive, and often fatal disease," says Jones, 59, best known for playing Cooter the mechanic on the hugely popular 1980s TV series "The Dukes of Hazzard." "I would drink anything I could get a hold of. Beer, wine, whiskey, you name it. Aqua Velva, if I didn't have anything else." Jones didn't know it then, but he was genetically predisposed to becoming an alcoholic, since the disease ran rampantly in both his mother and father's families. Jones grew up in Portsmouth, Virginia, an old shipbuilding town, and he lived in a railroad yard near the docks in a house that had no plumbing or electricity. Both his grandfathers and his father were railroad workers, the ones who built the tracks and trestles and spent long days driving spikes into crossties. His hard-working father never drank during the week, but come Friday evening he would break out the cheap whiskey and not stop drinking until late Sunday night. "He drank from the time he was 12 to the time he was 75," marvels Jones. "Once he retired at 65, he drank all day long, every day, so that his life was basically one long stupor." The elder Jones finally lapsed into a coma, and the doctors told Ben that his father was as good as dead. But the tough old man pulled out his coma, lived 6 more years, and never drank another drop. "He quit completely after 60 years of hard drinking," says Jones. "The lesson is that no matter how far gone somebody is, there is in every alcoholic the hope of sobriety."

It was a lesson that Jones would have to relearn all on his own. An inveterate dreamer with a touch of poet in him, Jones struggled through high school and skipped college to work in a series of dead-end jobs. "I had one job sticking the sticks into popsicles," he laughs. Finally he enrolled in college in Chapel Hill, North Carolina, and there he read philosophy, studied theater, got interested in politics—and drank like his heroes Dylan Thomas and Jack Kerouac. "Most people moderated that kind of behavior once they left college," he says. "But others of us were determined to set a new record for drinking." Jones made a decent living acting in summer stock productions, doing commercials, and filming bit parts in occasional movies. From the outside it looked like he was a successful, working actor, but up close it was clear that Jones was going nowhere. He was drinking more than ever, getting into fights with cops, going through three wives and countless bad relationships. "I got thrown in jail a lot for public drunkenness, disorderly conduct, stuff like that," he recalls. "One time, in Augusta, Georgia, I got busted and charged with 'Failure to Move On.' I guess you could say that was the story of my life."

Far from growing up and making progress, Jones was actually slipping backward, getting worse. And no matter how often his drinking landed him in jail, he convinced himself that he didn't have a problem. "The addict operates in this weird, insane state of denial," Jones says. "You know, if you eat asparagus and suddenly the asparagus makes you act crazy and fight with cops, you're going to stop eating asparagus pretty quick. But with addicts, it's always someone else's fault that you got in trouble. You tell yourself, 'Sure, I had a couple too many, but it won't happen again, so what's the problem?' And that is the power of the disease. The stuff is your boss, your God. The liquor has a contract out on you."

It took a brush with death to break through Jones's wall of denial. He was 36 years old and living alone in a small apartment in Atlanta. He had been divorced three times, and chased away most of his friends, even his fellow alcoholics. He spent all the money he made acting on booze. He didn't pay his bills and so the lights in his apartment were shut off. And then he went on a bender to end all benders—10 straight days of solid drinking. "I don't remember much of what happened, but I do know that I couldn't stop drinking," says Jones. "I was freefalling, out of control. I probably had enough booze in me to kill 10 people. Usually, I could stop drinking for a day or two and pull myself together. But this time it was different. I just could not stop drinking." Jones woke up one day gripped by terror, his body trembling uncontrollably, his mind filled with frightening visions. "I woke up laying on the floor, drenched in urine and vomit," he says. "I had the shakes and I was scared to death. What I really had was an acute case of alcohol poisoning, and it really should have killed me. And I remember thinking as I lay there on the floor, 'Man, you are dead right now.' "

Ben Jones could not fall any further than he did that night. All that was left for him to do was die. Years of drinking, of medicating his fears and insecurities with bottles of booze, had led to this pathetic scene in his ransacked, fetid apartment. He had failed, utterly and miserably, to find a way to live his life. And so he thought, as he lay in his waste, that he did not want to go on living. "Who would want to go on with a life like that?" he says.

Surely Ben Jones, son of railroad workers, had reached the end of the line.

•••

Then something strange and wonderful happened, something Jones will never be able to explain. "I lay there thinking, 'I don't want to live,' but then I thought, 'I don't want to die, either.' Beneath all of the self-loathing and crippling fear and destructive behavior, beneath all that there was this desperate will to live. There's a great quote from the philosopher Albert Camus: 'In the midst of winter I discovered there was within me an invincible summer.' " And though he hadn't said a prayer since he was a little boy, suddenly he felt the urge to pray. "I just said, 'Please, God, help me, I need help.' And from the second I uttered those words to this very moment 22 years later, I have not had a single drink of alcohol."

Miracles don't come with bolts of lightning or even flashes of great insight. They happen quietly, in dirty rooms, and often nobody notices until later. Certainly Jones wasn't thunderstruck by any great divine inspiration when he rose with great effort off the floor that day and placed his shaking hand on the phone. He wasn't thinking anything at all, he was simply trying to get from one moment in time to the next. And for some reason—he still doesn't know why—he figured that the way to survive was to dial the number of a friend, a fellow boozer. He did not know at the time that this friend was in Alcoholics Anonymous. But he knew instinctively that this friend might be able to help him. Sure enough, the friend came over and took him to an AA clubhouse in Atlanta. It was a plain room with a bed in it, a place where Jones could flop around and sweat the liquor out of his system. He didn't totally grasp the 12 steps of recovery right away, but he did do the important thing—he stopped drinking. Over time, Jones did subscribe to the program's powerful principles, but even today he prefers not to discuss his recovery program publically. "The whole point is to remain anonymous, to admit to yourself that there is a force that is greater and stronger than you," he will say. "And that realization was not that hard to come by. I looked around and I saw the sky and I saw the trees and I knew that I had not created these beautiful things myself. They were here when I showed up. Some other power created the world. And after I accepted that, the real payoff came. I found in sobriety the things that I had been seeking in intoxication: freedom from fear, freedom from doubt, freedom from feeling inferior. Then I began to experience the joy of life. And it was really like being reborn."

Not long after that fateful night, Jones saw his personality start to change. His confidence, his charisma, his sense of humor, his exuberance—all of these things began to bloom. Casting directors noticed it, too. Only a few months after he nearly died on the floor of his apartment, Jones auditioned for a role in a new TV series, about a pair of fast-driving, law-skirting good-old boys named Bo and Luke Duke. It was the biggest audition of his life, and he nailed it. Then, early in its very first season, "The Dukes of Hazzard" became the no. 1 show on TV. Just like that, Ben Jones was a celebrity, besieged on the street for autographs, and pulling down a cool $200,000 a year. "I was the guy who was filled with all this pity and self-loathing, and less than 2 years later I'm on the most popular show on TV!" says Jones, as if he still can't believe the turn his fortunes took. "And I'm trying to compute all of this, trying to make sense of it all. I mean, I had only done one thing differently, and that was not to drink."

The show ran from 1979 to 1985, and garnered for Jones the kind of fame that still gets him noticed on the street. Then, as if rising from the ashes of his alcoholism and becoming a wealthy TV star was not enough of a second act, Jones added another twist to his incredible story. In 1986 he defied all logic and decided to run for Congress. "No one in my district was going to challenge the incumbent, and it was something I felt needed to be done," says Jones, an old-fashioned, mainstream southern Democrat. Never mind that his checkered past was enough to derail a dozen campaigns. Jones figured he had nothing to hide and devised an unusual platform—honesty. "I used to say that I have more bones in my closet than the Smithsonian," says Jones. "I discovered that alcoholism is a disease people can relate to. It runs through many families and cuts across all the demographics. So people saw me as a person who had a serious problem and dealt with it successfully."

Jones lost that first race in 1986. He ran again in 1988 and caught a break when the incumbent, Pat Swindall, was indicted on federal perjury charges stemming from a money-laundering scheme. Incredibly, against all odds, Ben Jones was now a member of the U. S. Congress. On January 20, 1989, he attended the inauguration of newly elected President George Bush. "I go out there as a Congressman, and all the senators are there, and President Reagan is there, and the Washington monument is in front of me, and the Marine Corps Band is playing "America the Beautiful," and it's just this amazing, incredible, patriotic scene, and all of a sudden, standing there, that's when it hit me," Jones says. "Look how far I've been able to come, look where this old rummy ended up. And I realized my life was not about falling down, but about getting up."

Jones served 4 productive years, and even put up a good fight against Newt Gingrich before losing in 1994. Since then he has starred in two *Dukes of Hazzard* TV movies, and likes to tour with his band, the Cooter's Garage Band, singing classic country, bluegrass, and honky tonk tunes at fairs and festivals. Two years ago he opened a little roadside shrine to the series called Cooter's Place, at the foot of the Blue Ridge Mountains in picturesque Rappahannoch County, Virginia, where he lives with his fifth wife, Alma. "It was just this little fruit stand that we bought, and I filled it with all these scripts and costumes and 'Dukes' memorabilia that I had been lugging around, and I put a sign up that said 'Cooter's,' and that was all I did," he says. On grand-opening weekend, 6000 people showed up.

Sometimes, Ben Jones just has to sit and think about the miracle that is his life. "You have to be humble about it, and if you're not, something will remind you that you should be pretty quick," he says. "I know I am here by the grace of God, that for some reason I was given a second chance." That is why, every day, Jones feels the joy in whatever he does—a stroll, a hug, the sound of a singing bird. A big fan of philosophers like Kierkegaard, Jung, and, of course, Camus, Jones may not know why he survived, but he knows enough to savor every minute of his existence. "It's like the myth of Sisyphus," he explains. "The gods made him push that rock up the hill, and he'd get it to the top and it would roll back down. And he kept pushing it up and it would roll back down again. And what he did was find the *joy* in pushing that rock. He was like, 'Hey, look at me, I get to push this rock! I love it!' And that's how he tricked the gods, by finding the joy in life."

Above all, he knows he would not have this enlightened point of view—this ability to relish life on its own terms—had he not hit rock bottom. It took courage to get sober, courage to run for office, courage to confront his fears and replace them with faith—the kind of courage that Jones never knew he was capable of. "I look back and I actually have a certain amount of gratitude for my alcoholism," he says. "Would I like to not have been an alcoholic? That's like saying if frogs had wings they wouldn't bump their ass. Alcoholism is a part of me just like my fingerprints. And I have learned so much from dealing with this disease that it has enriched my life immeasurably. Now, I am able to help other people who are still sick and carry this message to those who need it. I like to tell them that I got sober the day before I died, and since then life has been a pretty miraculous thing."

Nowhere was that miracle more evident to Jones than in the simple of act of running. After achieving sobriety, he decided to go for a jog around his house, a distance of maybe 50 yards. "I collapsed in a heap, huffing and puffing, but I just couldn't believe that I had made it," he says. "To me, it was this amazing thing." The day he ran his very first mile was a truly miraculous day indeed, and not long after that he decided to enter the Peachtree 10K Run. He used to mock the hardy souls who ran the roughly 6-mile route; now he knew enough to admire their stamina and drive.

●●●

And so there he is, standing at the starting line, waiting for the gun to sound so he can finally run—so he can feel that *exhilaration* that is so new and strange to him. "On your mark!" he hears, and his freshly fit body slides into a runner's crouch. "Get set!" he hears, and his heart starts pounding a mile a minute. Then a gunshot, and there he goes, sprinting down Peachtree Street, the smile of a saved and grateful man splashed across his face. He runs freely, smoothly, confidently, not out in front of the pack but neither lagging behind it. Before he knows it, he is at the finish line, his face red from exertion, his body drenched in sweat. Yet he is not tired, not at all; in fact, he feels energized like never before. Not proud or cocky that he has finished, but happy that he is here at all. Still breathing, still pushing that rock up that hill—*still going.*

And so, heart pounding, he breaks clear of the crowd and starts to run again. He runs and runs, block after block, through the streets of Atlanta, further away from his past. He runs 1 mile and just keeps going; he hits 2 miles and he doesn't stop there. For most people the race is long over, but not for him.

Ben Jones still has a lot of running to do.

TIPS FOR TOUGH TIMES

The Ben Jones Story

*Failure is, in a sense, the highway to success,
inasmuch as every discovery of what is false leads
us to seek earnestly after what is true.*

John Keats

B en Jones knew that he was drinking himself to death,
and yet he couldn't stop. He had to literally bottom out
on the floor of his filthy apartment before he could find
his way out of the abyss. It took the redemptive power of total
and absolute failure to help him find the courage to fix what
was wrong. It took a frightening brush with death to teach
him how to live.

Addiction is a particularly insidious disease, but Jones's
story has a lesson for anyone who stumbles or fails on the way
to a goal. What he learned is that there is in everyone an
incredible capacity to overcome obstacles, no matter how
insurmountable those obstacles may appear. There is in
everyone an "invincible summer"—an opportunity to reinvent yourself into something better. Jones's family history was
filled with alcoholism, and yet he has bucked the odds to
become, in sobriety, the person he wanted to be. Whatever the
shackle that binds you, there is always hope that you can
break free.

1. **No One Is Predisposed to Fail** It would have been easy for Ben Jones to look back at his ancestors and assume he was doomed to be an alcoholic forever. In his case, it is true that the disease of alcoholism is hereditary and that he had an uphill battle to overcome his addictions. But the fact that he did proves that no one is bound by genealogy to act one way or another. *We all have within us the power to determine our own futures, to change the way we behave, and convincing ourselves otherwise is a crutch.*

2. **Know Enough to Ask for Help** For Ben Jones, the task of altering his behavior was something he simply couldn't handle by himself. After bottoming out, he sought counsel—from God, from a friend, from professionals. There is no shame in admitting defeat and asking for help; it is, for alcoholics, the first step toward recovery. The same holds for anyone who has fallen on hard times or otherwise hit a detour on the way to happiness. In times of trouble, humility may be the most important virtue. *Reaching out for a helping hand can be the most magnanimous thing we do for ourselves.*

3. **Find the Joy in Your Travails** Ben Jones related the story of Sisyphus, who tricked the gods by finding the joy in pushing a rock up a hill. Anyone can benefit from this approach. Jones learned that lesson the hard way—by almost dying. But anyone can put his or her problems

into context by assessing the positives in life. Appreciate the miracle of life, even when things aren't going as planned. For Jones, it was the simple act of running that filled him with a sense of joy. *No one should be so single-minded in pursuit of a goal that he or she forgets to savor the small blessings that life has to offer.*

13 HELPING HAND

The Patricia Biedar Story

I said, "I can't understand why I'm making these mistakes." And he said, "That's how you learn. That's how you really learn."

Pat Biedar

She said it one time, and only one time, and after that she forever banished the thought from her head. "I was on the phone with a business associate whom I didn't really know, and he casually asked me how I was doing," remembers Pat Biedar, the president of Priority Manufacturing, in Illinois. "And that's when I told him, 'I think I am ready to throw in the towel.' I had never, ever said that to anyone before. But at that point I just felt that I couldn't do this anymore, that I couldn't stop us from going down the tubes. I didn't know what else to do."

Biedar had good reason to feel desperate—her company was teetering on the brink of collapse. "Oh, we were a failing business, there's no doubt about that," she says. "We were all but gone." The problem wasn't that Biedar was a bad businesswoman. The problem was that she wasn't *any* kind of businesswoman at all. The circumstances that led her to take over Priority Manufacturing were tragic and unexpected, setting the stage for a remarkable case study in both crushing failure and soul-lifting success.

The tragedy had to do with Bruce Biedar, the handsome, self-assured man Pat met and fell in love with as a sophomore in Chicago's Steinmetz High School. The two dated for a couple of years and got married right after Pat graduated; within 6 years they had three children. Bruce went to work in the sheet-metal business, while Pat's principal job was to care for the kids. "That was the thing to do in those days: get married, have kids, stay at home, and take care of them," she says. "And I really liked doing it." Still, she always found time to work, as a secretary to earn pocket money, and later, as a travel agent, to help further her dream. Once her kids were good and grown, Biedar planned on starting her own travel agency. "I spent 3 years studying the industry, learning about computers and sales and all that," she says. "I was going to buy my own agency, and Bruce was 100 percent behind me."

In the meantime, Biedar's husband—"a very hard worker and a natural leader," she says—rose to the rank of vice president of a sheet-metal company. But then he got the urge to strike out on his own. "He would say, 'As long as I have to work this hard and this many hours, I might as well be working for myself,' " says Biedar. "So we took our life savings, personally guaranteed some loans, pledged our house, and started Priority Manufacturing."

There was a great deal of risk involved; the economy was sluggish, interest rates were sky high, and the very house in which they lived was at stake should they fail. But Bruce Biedar believed in his business, and Pat believed in Bruce. The company—which made precision metal fabrications such as laser cutters and welders—got off to a terrible start: some crucial equipment being delivered to their plant fell off a crane and broke. It took months to replace the equipment, and drained the Biedar's emergency fund of every single penny. "That was traumatic," she recalls. "But the second year we bounced right back."

Biedar wasn't just a sideline cheerleader. Early on, she pitched in by working as the company's janitor. But once her husband recognized her talents, her role in the company quickly grew. Data entry, purchasing, filing, receptionist duty—Pat Biedar did it all. And, as her children grew older, she began working longer and longer hours at the plant, topping 65 hours most weeks. "Bruce ran the shop, and I was involved in the office side of things," she says. "But I watched him work and learned a great deal about him as a man. I was impressed with his positive attitude, his aggressiveness, the way he cared about people, the way his workers respected him. I learned that in business you have to be a tough cookie." Priority Manufacturing hit another snag in 1984, 4 years after it got off the ground. A big delivery was shipped to China, but got hung up in customs. The expected inflow of cash never happened, and suddenly things were tight again. The setback happened right around the time that Biedar had finally decided to buy her own travel agency. She had already scouted a couple of locations when all of a sudden Priority slipped back into crisis mode. "So I put my plans on the back burner," she says. "Bruce loved the idea of me opening an agency, and he really pushed me in that direction. But I said, 'How can you tell me to go and do it when we're struggling with the company?' I told him I was staying to concentrate on the business. I told him, 'Don't worry, I can always open an agency.'"

Biedar and her husband weathered the storm and got the company back on solid ground. But the chance to pursue her own dream was about to disappear.

●●●

The Chicago Bears were playing a big game, and the Chicago Biedars were planning a big party. They invited several friends to come watch the game and barbecue some burgers and franks. The morning of the shindig "we were very excited about it," remembers Pat. "There were no signs that anything was wrong."

Biedar normally accompanied her husband to the health club every morning at 7:00 a.m. But that September day Bruce decided to work out of the house, since Priority Manufacturing was in the process of moving to a new, larger location. "I told him, 'Stay at home and work from here, where it will be more quiet,'" says Biedar. "Then I went to the bank to get some change–of-address forms for the business." An hour or so later, Biedar was on her way to the plant when she decided to drop by the house and pay her husband a quick visit. "As soon as I walked in I heard him calling for me," she says. "I ran upstairs and I saw him there, and he said, 'Pat, I am really sick.'"

Biedar called the paramedics, but by the time they got there it was too late. "Bruce died in my arms," she says. "I worked on him until the paramedics got me out of there. He had a blood clot and it burst his heart." The heart attack, says Biedar, "was a terrific shock, out of the blue, something we never talked about or prepared for. I was really not ready for what I had to do next." Her husband's tragic death could not have come at a worse time: the company was not only moving but expanding, and selling it would be next to impossible. "All our machinery was on a truck, disconnected," she says. "The building we were in had already been sold. We had no location and we had this widow's price tag on the whole business. Basically I felt it was unsellable at any reasonable price. Plus I had to make a decision very, very quickly." There was no way that Biedar would let the company her husband had worked so hard to create slip through her fingers without a fight. "I had to go forward," she says. "We were tripling our size and doubling our overhead, and I was totally unprepared to man-age all that. But what else could I do? The only choice I had was to go forward." And so Pat Biedar, with no business training what-soever, became the boss at Priority Manufacturing.

She was 43 years old.

One thing Biedar did have was the wholehearted support of her children. Her eldest daughter, Patte, at the time a 21-year-old pastry chef, even agreed to come aboard to help run the plant. Pat's central mission was to drum up new business, and keep the old business, in order to keep the company in the black. It proved to be a terribly uphill battle. "The market was very slow," says Biedar. "We lost some customers. And the customers who stayed were not as confident as I would have liked them to be. The sheet-metal business was pretty much a boy's club back then, so a lot of the customers were evaluating me and sort of taking bets. 'Let's see how long she lasts,' that sort of thing." Looking back, Biedar can hardly blame anyone for being skeptical about her chances. "I did-n't know what I was doing," she concedes. "I tried to analyze things, but I couldn't figure it out. It's not that I wasn't trying hard enough, it's that I didn't have the knowledge. It's hard to be a leader when you don't know what you're doing."

Bieder expected things to be tough, but she never dreamed they'd be as tough as they were. Customers were dropping Priority one after the other. New business? No such luck. To make mat-ters worse, many of the company's employees were running amok. "I didn't know enough about sheet-metal manufacturing to know if they were really working or just goofing off," Biedar says. "And a lot of them just didn't respect me, didn't respect a woman run-ning things, much less the wife of the boss. So there was a lot of insubordination."

Still stinging from the death of her husband, Biedar had to endure open hostility from her own employees. "I would tell someone directly to do something, and they would say something smart to me and not do it. They would be flippant and cynical, and they would say things to my face and behind my back." Biedar might have been devastated by such blatant disrespect, had she had the time to feel anything. "Oh, I cried and prayed a lot in the beginning," she says. "But after a while I stopped crying. I was just too involved in keeping everything afloat. I had to forget the tears."

But no matter what she did, she couldn't stop the company's assets from dwindling away. She was taking no salary, and she had pledged everything she owned to keep the business going. And still the months passed without any indication that Priority's fortunes would improve. "Everything was on the line," Biedar says. "If I didn't make it, I would lose everything that my husband and I had worked for. And that included our house." The stress took its toll on Biedar, who had never really had a proper chance to grieve for her husband. "I was working 60, 70 hours a week. I would come home and go to bed right away, and then I would wake up at 2:00 a.m." Her precious few moments of sleep were interrupted by thoughts of what she needed to do back at the plant. "If it were up to me I would have gone right back to work at 2:00 a.m., when I woke up," she says. "But my children would not allow me to go to work until the sun came up." And so Biedar would sit in her bedroom, in the darkness, wide awake and worried to death. And then, at the first hint of sunlight, she would get in the car and go right back to work.

The banks were calling in her loans. The company was essentially broke. The customer base had shrunk nearly to nonexistence. Worst of all, there was absolutely no reason to hope that things would get better anytime soon. Eighteen months had passed since her husband had died, and Biedar sensed the end was near for the company they had built together. "I kept up a good face, this facade that I was doing okay," she says. "I never let anyone know the real facts, I didn't want people to know that we were struggling. But at the same time I knew that there was pretty much no chance of anything good happening for me." One day a client was on his way from Biedar's facility to another company, and asked her to call ahead and let the company's owner know he was on his way. Biedar obliged, and made small talk with the owner, a man she barely knew. "He asked me how I was doing," Biedar says. "And that was the first time I said, 'I am ready to throw in the towel.' I had never told that to anyone else. But he asked, and for some reason I told him the truth."

● ● ●

The owner's response was swift and clear. "He said, 'I don't want to hear you say that,'" remembers Biedar. "He knew that I had taken over the company after Bruce died, but he didn't know much else. But right away he said that all owners were at one time in the same boat as me. And the one thing you never do is quit. So forget about throwing in the towel."

The owner offered Biedar a deal—he would send over a friend, a retired CPA and the owner of a manufacturing company, to evaluate her business. If he felt that the company couldn't survive, then Biedar could close its doors. She agreed, and opened up the plant and its books for inspection. The former CPA spent a solid week at Priority, looking for hints that it could survive. His conclusion? "He said it was a viable company," says Biedar. "I knew that it was, that my husband had created something sound. The problem was that I personally didn't have the tools to make it work. I told him, 'I can't understand why I'm making all these mistakes.' And he said, 'That's how you learn. That's how you *really* learn.'"

The friendly colleague and the former CPA accepted a fee for the services—believing it was the only way she would take their advice seriously—but they allowed Biedar to pay them over 4 years. The real reason they agreed to help, though, was because they believed it was the way the business world should work. With their assistance, Biedar learned about business plans, budgets, contracts, job descriptions, performance evaluations—everything it takes to run a business. Slowly but surely, the overwhelming sense of dread and anxiety began to lift. "It took a long time, but we saw positive signs along the way," says Biedar. "We knew that if we really put in the effort, if we really focused on one goal, we would see results. And that was such a good feeling." Installing a computer system alone greatly improved the company's efficiency. Then Biedar started trimming the fat. She fired insubordinate employees and got rid of several contractors who were not helpful. "We cleaned house big time," she says. "And after that the mood in the company started lifting." Not long after she first admitted she wanted to quit the business, Biedar knew she would never feel such crippling self-doubt again. "I never, ever said I would quit after that phone call," she recalls. "Things were bad at the company for a long time after that, and there were many times when I would look at things and say, 'Oh my God, now what?' But I never, ever again said that I wanted to quit the business. The words that I used totally changed. When something went wrong I would say, 'Somehow, we're going to get through this. I can't tell you today how we're going to do it, but check back with me tomorrow and I will find a way.'"

Emboldened, Biedar corrected some key mistakes. Priority stopped taking orders that weren't profitable, something poor accounting had led them to do. They also diversified into new markets such as agricultural and trucking parts. "My daughter, Patte, proved to be a terrific businesswoman, and she became my right arm," says Biedar. "Without her, I don't think we would have made it." Yes, there were bumps on the comeback road, but Pat Biedar was sleeping a heck of a lot better than before. "I wasn't getting up at 2:00 a.m. anymore," she says. "When you don't have the stress of not knowing if you're going to be around tomorrow, it's a lot easier to sleep." In 1991, 5 years after her husband died, Priority Manufacturing went back into the black. "That was a wonderful feeling," Biedar says. "I was the one who had taken it into the red, and now I had brought it back. We still had our ups and downs after that, but even then we had a plan in place. We had a structure. We knew what it was that we had to do."

Considering how close the company was to total ruin just a few years ago, its turnaround is truly a miracle born of courage and perseverance. Today, Priority Manufacturing is a strong and stable company filled with happy and resourceful employees. In 1995 Priority won a Blue Chip Award, recognizing it as one of the top companies in Illinois and, indeed, the country. Biedar and her family were flown to Washington, D.C., where they got to visit the White House and meet with congressmen. "That was the one moment where I honestly could say that I felt like somebody, I felt *special*," says Biedar. "Before that I was just too busy working to think about that, but here was an award that said, 'You have done something, you have struggled, and you have achieved.' Our company came out of nowhere, against all odds, and look at us now. And that really made me feel special."

That day, Pat Biedar, the woman who refused to throw in the towel, got up and gave a speech. "I talked about how, no matter what, you can never quit. I almost did, believe me, I came very close. But the most important thing I did was turn to others for help. To admit failure is really tough for anyone. But what I said in my speech is that we should not look at failure that way. Failing isn't the worst thing in the world, not by a long shot. It may be at the time, but when you look back, failure is what teaches you how to succeed. All you have to do is keep moving forward, and do the best you can. And that's just what I did."

Occasionally, people will ask Pat Bieder what her husband would think of her performance. It is not a question she ever asks herself. "When he died, I used to think, 'What would Bruce have said?'" she says. "But not anymore. Now, it's me. I am doing this for me and my family. For the company, and for the employees. It's no longer an issue of me doing it for him." Then Biedar pauses, and a smile washes over her face. "I do know one thing, though" she finally says. "And that is that Bruce would be *very* proud of me."

TIPS FOR TOUGH TIMES

The Pat Biedar Story

Good people are good because they've come to wisdom through failure. We get very little wisdom from success.

William Saroyan

Sometimes we seek out great challenges in our lives. Sometimes the challenges find us. Pat Biedar never expected to be running her husband's company, but she was forced by circumstance to do it. And the humiliating failure she experienced could have easily led her to sell the company she and her husband worked so hard to create. Instead, she chose to stick it out and learn from her mistakes, and eventually she turned her fortunes around.

Biedar's path to success was humbling and eye-opening. She learned a great deal about how to run a business, but she learned even more about how to run her life. Biedar's story shows that there is much to gain from failure, as long as we stay attuned to the lessons it offers. It's remarkable how many people who have experienced failure—Pat Biedar included— say they wouldn't trade their struggles for anything in the world.

1. **Take the Blame When It Belongs to You** Pat Biedar didn't have to look far to figure out why her company was failing—Priority Manufacturing's anemic bottom line was all the proof she needed. But when her employees turned on her and her clients abandoned her, she could have faulted them and absolved herself of blame. Instead, she admitted that her lack of business experience was the central reason her company was failing. Admitting that was difficult and painful, but a necessary first step toward turning the tide. *When things go wrong, don't look for alibis and excuses; accept the blame, admit your faults, and figure out how to fix things.*

2. **Don't Be Afraid to Make Mistakes** Bieder's ordeal taught her many things, but perhaps the most important was the value of mistakes. Conventional thinking holds that mistakes are bad, but in fact they are the best and fastest way to learn a lesson. At first, Biedar felt the humiliating stigma of failure, but after a while she realized that failure is not the worst thing that can happen—not by a long shot. Every mistake she made—and she made plenty—was instrumental in her business education. *The fear of making mistakes should never stop you from taking chances, since every mistake is an instant and invaluable lesson.*

3. **When All Seems Lost, Turn to Others for Help** Biedar's company was as close to collapsing as it could be, and no one

would have blamed her for folding up her tent. Wisely, though, she took one final step before that drastic action—she accepted outside help. Sometimes all it takes is a pair of fresh eyes to put your problems in perspective. And, more often than not, people are anxious to share the wisdom they have earned through experience. Not taking advantage of the help that is out there for the taking is a terrible waste. *Doing the best you can isn't always enough; when things seem hopeless, don't be afraid to ask for help.*

14 GIANT KILLER

The Bill Pilczuk Story

All I think about is doing my best. But I always think that my best is good enough to win.

Bill Pilczuk

They rented the convention hall in Cape May, New Jersey, and they threw up some banners and signs and balloons. They advertised in the local papers, and they mentioned it to everyone they knew. They decided to make it a Beer and Beef Night, and they got a band to bang out rock-and-roll music. Craig and Kathleen Pilczuk expected a decent crowd to turn out on that January night. What they got was 1500 people—at $10 a pop—crammed into the hall.

And all to help this local kid live out his crazy dream.

Of course, it wasn't just any dream—it was a dream to make the U.S. Olympic Swimming Team. And it wasn't just any kid, it was Bill Pilczuk, the scrawny overachiever who came late to the sport of swimming, received no scholarships out of high school, and won not a single swimming title during his college years. A real Cinderella story, this Pilczuk boy, but still, there wasn't a swimmer out there who worked any harder or had more confidence. "Bill approaches every race like it's two kids swimming in a backyard pool," says Dean Hutchinson, a fellow swimmer and, for years, Pilczuk's training partner. "He doesn't care who he's swimming against, he feels that he should beat them."

And so there was electricity in the air that night in late 1995, when 1500 believers gathered to raise funds for a native son. Pilczuk himself, then 23, wore a big smile as he worked the crowd, shaking hands, thanking people, accepting good wishes, giving a speech. "Everyone was being so nice to me, I felt like it was my wedding night," says Pilczuk, now 28. "It was really a good feeling because I didn't realize that many people were even aware that I swam." The event raised enough money to support Pilczuk for a full year, enough that he could forgo a job and train full time for the Olympics in 1996. He thought of all his boosters back home as he traveled to Indianapolis for the Olympic time trials, for the chance to make the team as one of only two 50-meter swimmers. The Cinderella story was on the verge of its happy ending.

But it did not play out that way. Bill Pilczuk did not make the Olympic team. He finished third by the excruciating margin of five hundredths of a second. *Five hundredths of a second!* Word got back to the faithful in Cape May: the kid was out. The dream was dashed. Forget the parade.

So much, it seemed, for fairytales.

• • •

It was the kind of heartbreaking loss that could send even strong men into spirals of self-doubt. "A lot of my friends quit the sport right after losing in the Olympic trials," says Pilczuk. "A lot of people with way more talent than me retired after not making the team." Who would have blamed Pilczuk, no spring chicken at 23, for doing the same?

In fact, Bill Pilczuk never thought of giving up, not even for a moment. He simply wasn't the type to quit, never had been. Swimming was a part of him now, the thing that defined who he was. He felt comfortable in the water; after all, he grew up in a coastal resort town, and spent his childhood frolicking in the Atlantic. "I got pulled out in a couple of undertows," he recalls, "and that teaches you how to swim pretty quick." Sure, he was already 11 years old when he signed up for his first official lesson, taking up the sport only after his grandmother suggested he needed a winter activity to go with his little league baseball. But didn't he excel at swimming almost from the very start? And, yes, he was by his own admission a "crap swimmer" in high school. But his body was strong and his technique was good and his arms were as long as rowboat oars. "Today my wingspan is about 6 feet 8 inches," says Pilczuk, who stands 6 feet 4 inches. "It helps if your arms are a lot longer than your body because then your paddles are in the water longer."

More important than his natural affinity for swimming was Pilczuk's ability to shrug off defeat. No college offered him a scholarship out of high school, and when he visited swimming powerhouse Indian River Junior College in Florida "they kind of laughed at my times," he says. "They flatly told me I wasn't fast enough to go there." So Pilczuk went to nearby Miami Dade, and improved enough to transfer to Division I Auburn University as a junior walk-on. Still, he had to pay his own tuition, and when he went to the NCAA championships as an alternate, all he got to do was grab a towel and dry off the starting blocks for his teammates. None of that, however, was enough to discourage him. Now swimming the 50 meters exclusively, he had an explosive burst off the blocks and felt he was as fast as anyone for the first 25 meters. "I was making drops in my time every year," he says. "I was making progress, and that's what kept me going."

After college he kept swimming, living off what little he had left from a couple of student loans. "I had a part-time sales job at a Gold's Gym," he says. "I had just enough money to buy cans of spaghetti and to hit the all-you-can-eat pizza buffet." His sacrifices paid off when, in 1994, he beat Olympian John Olsen and earned a spot at the World Championships in Rome. The Worlds were a huge opportunity for him, and Pilczuk let his nerves get the best of him. Normally a good sleeper before meets, he "was up all night before the race," he recalls. "I was seeded third going in and I finished eleventh. I got killed." Back in Auburn, he had no money, no coach, no training program—it seemed like another ideal time to hang up his goggles. Instead, he and his pal Dean Hutchinson came up with their own program and pushed each other even harder. "No one in the swimming world knew who we were, and no one should have known us," says Hutchinson. "But we took it personally anyway, and we wanted people to know that we worked harder than anyone else. We felt that no one out there had the right to beat us."

Pilczuk saw the 1996 games as a chance to finally shine. The Beer and Beef Night in Cape May increased his confidence, and while no one ranked him among the six top candidates for the two 50-meter spots, he felt he had a solid chance to make the team. Then, at the morning session of the 1-day Olympic time trial in Indianapolis, Pilczuk swam his best time ever—22.52 seconds— and was seeded third going into the finals. Another strong swim that afternoon, and the dream might finally come true.

But once again the pressure proved too much for Pilczuk. He had slept only 3 hours the previous night, and hoped to get some rest between the morning and afternoon races. "But I was so nervous I couldn't take my nap," he recalls. "Standing on the blocks

I was so tired that I felt numb." He got off to a great start and was leading the race at the halfway mark, but after that he lost steam and finished third by five hundredths of a second. He missed going to the Olympics by all of .05. "It really wasn't a crushing defeat," Pilczuk insists. "I felt worse when I got back home and everyone said to me, 'Gee, you finished third, too bad.' And I was like, 'Hey, I finished third, that's pretty good!' No one gave me much of a shot anyway." Missing out on the Olympics, says his friend Dean Hutchinson, "was definitely disappointing. Not that Bill is the kind of guy who's going to sulk and not talk to his girl-friend or things like that. But I'm sure that the loss drove him to get better."

In fact, the heartbreaking defeat did a number on Pilczuk's psyche, jarring him out of his set routine. Right after the meet, he and a buddy boarded a plane for Breckenridge, Colorado, where for the first time ever Bill Pilczuk went skiing. He had not allowed himself to try the sport because he feared an injury, but now he threw all caution to the wind. "I said, 'Hey, I'm done swimming, I'll do whatever I want, I just don't care,' " he recalls. "I wrecked pretty hard a couple of times, but I figured if I got hurt, I could always rehab and come back. I just didn't care anymore, and I had a really great time." Hurtling down the slopes at breakneck speed gave Pilczuk a new perspective on his swimming. "My new outlook was, 'I'm just going to go out there and swim, I'm not going to let swimming rule my life,' " he explains. "I'm not going to take naps all the time, stuff like that. I'm just going to let it all hang out. It was a very liberat-ing thing to do."

Pilczuk's decision to take some pressure off himself paid off handsomely. He won a competition in France and picked up enough cash to keep training. He went to the National Championships in 1996 and won a gold medal; the next year, he won the Nationals again. That second time, he beat swimmers who had made the Olympic squad, and he set a new personal best, at 22.41. To top it all off, he qualified to swim at the 1998 World Championships in Perth, Australia, in what would be his biggest, most important meet to date. No doubt, he was a huge underdog going into the Worlds. In the United States, Pilczuk was well respected but hardly a superstar. Internationally, he was an absolute nobody. Few people gave him any chance to pick up a medal in Perth, much less beat the overwhelming favorite— Alexander Popov, the towering, intimidating Russian who for several years had been the world's best swimmer, unbeaten in major competitions, unchallenged in his supremacy. What hope did a skinny overachiever like Pilczuk have against a giant like that?

• • •

Alexander Popov is 6 feet 8 inches and weighs well over 200 pounds. His body is thick and muscular, his calves as big as 10-gallon jugs. His wide face is creased by an imposing set of eyebrows, and his standard expression is a menacing scowl. In the ready room before races most swimmers joke around to alleviate the tension; Popov utters not a word and stares down his opponents. In his prime he was, quite simply, unconquerable. "I look like a little kid next to him," laughs Pilczuk, who tops out at 180 pounds. "He really carries himself in an awe-inspiring way."

Pilczuk would have you believe that he was sufficiently awed by Popov to put any thought of beating him out of his head. "I had my sights set on the silver," he swears. "A bronze would have been fine, too. What I really wanted was to leave there with a medal." But his good friend Dean Hutchinson says that Pilczuk "downplays his competitiveness. He didn't do anything like put a sign on his locker that said, 'I'm going to beat Alexander Popov.' But he did put a picture of Popov in his locker, long before he ever got the chance to race him. You see, Bill gets offended when people don't think he's as fast as he is."

Sure enough, the day of the Worlds, everyone was talking about Michael Klim, the strong Australian swimmer who was given the best chance of beating Popov. Nobody, not a soul, was buzzing about Bill Pilczuk. To no one's surprise, he went out in the morning race and swam poorly. The same old problems were bugging him again. He hadn't slept well the night before, and he was totally bushed. Any minute now, he'd start feeling the old familiar pressure again. He went back to his hotel room and laid down for a nap.

Strangely, he didn't feel nervous at all; in fact he felt calm and relaxed. Before he knew it he was fast asleep, and he didn't wake up until 3 hours later. "I mean I really conked out," he says. "When I opened my eyes I was like, 'Whoa, what day is it?' I had never ever slept like that before a race." When he got up he felt refreshed, as if all was right with his world. The nap, it turned out, was only his first lucky break. When he went down to the hotel restaurant—a place where he had eaten some truly ghastly meals—he took a chance and asked the chef if he could whip up a pasta dish not on the menu. The chef said sure, and minutes later Pilczuk downed the most delicious dish of pasta he'd ever had. Then he went to the pool for his afternoon warm-up, shivering with cold since the clouds had blocked the sun. But as soon as he hit the water, the sun suddenly appeared, heating him for what became an excellent prerace warm-up. His final lucky break occurred when he got his lane assignment; he would be in lane 6 and Popov in lane 4. "That meant he wouldn't be able to see me," says Pilczuk. "If Popov sees you, he's going to beat you, simple as that."

Pilczuk climbed up on his block and once again felt strangely serene. "All I'm thinking is, 'I'm going to get to that wall as fast as I can,'" he says. The starting beep sounded and he got off to his customary quick start, accelerating the instant he sliced into the water. One of the few 50-meter swimmers who does not surface for a breath, Pilczuk focused on the bottom of the pool and poured everything he had into his first 25 meters. At the halfway mark he was well in front, at least a half-length ahead of Alexander Popov. At 35 meters, he was still leading, but Popov was clearly gaining on him. "I died with maybe six strokes to go," says Pilczuk. "My tempo slowed down and I wasn't catching any water. That's when the others started reeling me in." Pilczuk, spent and needing air, dug down deep for the final six strokes and finally touched the wall. He looked up at the scoreboard overhead, waiting an eternity until the times were flashed. Then he saw them, in a stark, yellow digital display:

Pilczuk, USA, 22.29
Popov, Russia, 22.43

It dawned on him in a wondrous instant: he had beaten Popov. Cheers and screams filled the air, but Pilczuk didn't hear them. "I wasn't aware of anything around me, except for the fact that I had won." Soon enough, his blissful numbness was shattered by a cry from the stands: "Way to go, Billy! Way to go!" It was Pilczuk's mom.

Back in the United States, all the papers reported on the miracle upset down under. "Bill beat the giant, he was the only one to beat the giant," Dean Hutchinson says with obvious pride. "No one had touched out Popov in something like 7 years, and Bill did it. He is still the only person to have beaten Popov at the Worlds or the Olympics." Most amazing to Hutchinson is the distance his friend traveled to get to this history-making moment. "Coming out of high school he was about as low on the totem pole as you could be. And to think that he would even qualify to swim at a Division 1 college, much less beat the best swimmer in the world—a *million* people would have told you there was just no way."

And so the folks in Cape May got out the banners and balloons, and rented out the very same convention hall again. Three fire engines escorted Pilczuk from the cracked and rundown elementary school pool where he got his start to the site of his second party, this one even more full of hope and happiness than the first. Pilczuk once again worked the crowd, shaking hands, saying thanks—and this time signing autographs. Not far from the hall, at the end of a mall, the town erected a giant sign. It read, simply: *BILL PILCZUK—WORLD'S FASTEST SWIMMER.*

How had he done it, this scrawny overachiever who had so many chances to quit? How had he managed to rebound from the debacle of the Olympic time trials? Throughout his career, Pilczuk took pride in his approach to swimming—instead of focusing on what place he finished, he concentrated only on improving his times. "If my goal was to drop .2 from my time, and I did that and finished fourth, then I was happy with my performance," he explains. But the fact remained that at big meets he'd feel the pressure to win. Time and again he would tense up; inevitably he'd sleep badly the night before. Finally, after missing out on the Olympics by only .05, he truly shifted his focus away from winning races. "That allowed me to be less intense about what I was doing," says Pilczuk. "I was still completely dedicated to swimming, but I stopped worrying about the outcome of races. When you worry about outcomes, you're worrying about something you can't control, about how other people perform. I just worry about my own lane and let the clock work itself out." Behind this new, zenlike approach was the same old confidence. "All I think about is doing my best," he says. "But I always think that my best is good enough to win."

Once Pilczuk's never-say-die attitude was crossed with the wisdom only defeat brings, he was able to slay the giant—to reach his true potential. Today, he still gives speeches about his triumph, letting fans touch his shiny gold medal, and urging them to always follow their dreams. "You are never too old to get it done," he says. "If I had quit when I was 21, look what I would have missed. Instead I just kept going and going and finally got really good." After his victory, a sponsor approached him about creating a Bill Pilczuk poster, and asked him to come up with a slogan. Pilczuk gave it lots of thought, and finally figured out what he wanted the poster to say. It was a single word: *RELENTLESS.*

TIPS FOR TOUGH TIMES

The Bill Pilczuk Story

Whatever we succeed in doing is a transformation of something we have failed to do.

Paul Valéry

Not many people gave Bill Pilczuk any chance to beat the best swimmer in the world. He was too old, they said, and too slow—not to mention too tightly wound and too unknown and too inexperienced and too everything else. In fact, he may have been all of those things, but he was also too sure of his own abilities to pay much attention to what they were saying. And, in the end, Pilczuk's opinion of his talents was the only one that mattered.

Pilczuk's confidence was tested many times, but none of his failures ever dented his belief in himself. He responded to his setbacks by addressing his major flaws and changing his strategy, all while working harder than ever. His achievement—rising from near obscurity to beat the fastest swimmer in the world—was truly an epic achievement, but the lesson of his story applies to small-scale goals and dreams as well. We all have the potential to overcome long odds, but not unless we believe in our hearts that we can slay the giant.

1. **A Million-to-One Odds Means You Have a Shot** There will always be people around who will dismiss your dream, and

the more ambitious the dream, the more they will deride it. But their assessments lack one crucial bit of information—the level of your determination to succeed. Why listen to someone who doesn't know the complete story? Long odds only mean that something is difficult to achieve: if it were impossible, there wouldn't be any odds at all. Bill Pilczuk's past failures may have convinced others that he couldn't beat Alexander Popov, but Pilczuk knew better. *No matter how poor your track record or how long the odds, as long as you're in the game you always have a shot.*

2. **Don't Focus on the Prize, Focus on the Process** Pilczuk analyzed his failures and saw that he always tightened up before big races. Somehow he had to find a way to overcome his anxiety, and he did that by shifting his focus away from winning. Instead, he focused on his performance, on executing the race as efficiently as he could. His desire to win was not diminished in any way, but the change in strategy took some of the pressure off. Thus, Pilczuk's victory over Popov might never have happened had he not failed in previous races and been forced to shift his focus. *When the pressure begins to mount, concentrate on your performance and not on the result.*

3. **You Are Never Too Old to Overcome Failure** Pilczuk was, at 27, a grizzled veteran in the world of swimming. Some peo-

ple even considered him over the hill. That's why almost no one gave him a chance to beat Popov. But courage and resolve know no age limit. A lifetime of failures can be erased with one spectacular success. *Others may underestimate you because of your age, but as long as you're breathing, you have a chance to pull off a miracle.*

15 HUBBLE TROUBLE

The Earl Stafford Story

Adversity is just the dues you pay to get into the club.

Earl Stafford

Nights were hardest for Earl Stafford, loving husband, father of three, and failed businessman. At night, Stafford would bolt up in bed and stare into the darkness for endless hours, wondering how things could have ever come to this. Sometimes he felt so bad he'd rush to the bathroom and throw up; other times his body shook uncontrollably. Always, day and night, his stomach turned and twisted into painful knots. "That was a very, very, very stressful time," says Stafford, 52. "There's not a lot of happiness in your life when something like that happens. Not a lot of joy."

Stafford can smile about his ordeal now, but it's the kind of smile that says he hasn't forgotten the pain. He is tall and handsome and built like a running back, and he ambles around his elegant suite of offices in Fairfax, Virginia, with a looseness and confidence born of great success. His remarkable company, Universal Systems & Technology, Inc., which is known as UNITECH, has revenues of more than $40 million a year, and Stafford is routinely referred to as one of the nation's most astute entrepreneurs. Yet there isn't a trace of arrogance in his boisterous disposition; indeed, he is humble about how far he has come. That's because, only a few short years ago, Stafford's situation was so calamitous that he could not pay his bills. One day they shut off the lights in his house. Next they turned off his telephone. "Christmas comes around and I can't get any presents for the children," says Stafford. "Hardship and struggle became a way of life."

And all because of this little glitch in the Hubble space telescope.

The truth is, Earl Stafford never saw it coming. Up until one terrible week in 1990, when his world collapsed, his fortunes had been on a steady, upward trajectory, thanks largely to his strong work habits. One of 12 children born in a small, working-class New Jersey town, Stafford grew up without a lot of money but with plenty of ideas about how to earn some. "Being broke deals with your wallet, but being poor deals with your attitude," says Stafford. "My family didn't have much money, but we were never allowed to think of ourselves as poor." Instead, the Stafford kids scraped up cash however they could: running paper routes, cutting grass, mowing lawns. "I couldn't wait for it to snow," says Stafford. "Why, so I could go skiing? No, so I could make money shoveling snow. I'd go downtown and make $25 a day. That's what you did, and that's what you were expected to do."

After high school, Stafford enlisted in the Air Force, one of his smartest moves. "One thing the military does well is reward performance quickly," he says. "I worked hard and there was an instant payoff." Stafford trained as an air traffic controller, served as an assistant liaison officer to the Federal Aviation Administration, and earned a reputation as a leader. The Air Force helped him get his bachelor's degree from the University of Massachusetts, then an MBA from Southern Illinois. He was set up for a long and fruitful career in the military.

But Stafford had other ideas. For one thing, he had gotten married and had a child, Earl Jr., and supporting his family on a less than staggering military allowance was getting harder and harder. Then there was his burning desire to go into business for himself. So, after 20 years, 1 month, and 17 days in the military—and after racking up some $15,000 in debt—Stafford became a civilian. He accepted a job with RVA, a small company that provided training for the FAA. Not surprisingly, he thrived. "It wasn't about me being smart, it was about me working hard," he recalls. "I'm there until 8, 9, 10 o'clock at night, and on weekends, and the big shots aren't. So I got to know this training system better than anyone in the company." Seizing the moment, Stafford took his expertise and quit, offering to come back as an independent contractor. In 1988, Stafford's brand new company, UNITECH, was hired by RVA.

It took a while for his gutsy move to pay off. Early on, he had only one $23,655 contract from the Navy, and could barely afford to cut himself a meager weekly paycheck. But then, in 1990, Stafford snagged a $300,000 subcontract for NYMA, Inc. a high-tech company that was working for the National Aeronautics and Space Administration on its mammoth Hubble space telescope project. Stafford was hired to provide a support staff for the team of scientists handling the launch. Expectations for the 11-ton, school-bus-sized telescope were sky high at NASA, and Stafford couldn't help but get caught up in the frenzy. "When I got the Hubble job, I said to myself, 'Man, you have finally arrived,'" Stafford recalls. "This was the Hubble telescope! One of the biggest launches NASA ever had! I thought the contract was only going to expand, and I started looking to hire more and more people." Stafford rented and furnished his own offices, and finally allowed himself to draw a reasonable salary. "Things are happening, things are really looking good," he says. "After all these years I'm finally on easy street. What could possibly go wrong?"

• • •

Several miles up in space, something did go wrong. One of the mirrors aboard the Hubble malfunctioned, and the first few images sent back to Earth were hopelessly out of focus. Soon, newspapers were filled with stories about how the Hubble was a bust. "I would read about it in the papers and hear about it on TV, just like everybody else," Stafford says. "And I would think, 'Uh oh, this can't be good.' " Still, he had no idea how bad it could be. NASA quickly scaled back the expensive Hubble program, and began cutting contracts. Stafford was one of the first to get the call that he was gone. Losing the Hubble deal was a devastating blow, but, Stafford told himself, it wasn't the end of the world. At least he still had that little contract with RVA, and that, after all, was better than nothing.

Then, a few days later, Stafford's telephone rang again.

This time it was someone at RVA calling with more bad news. RVA's contract had been called in, and, in turn, it instantly terminated its subcontract with UNITECH. The timing was purely coincidental, but the fact remained that in one single week Stafford's world had been turned upside down. In a span of days he went from a promising businessman on the brink of life-changing success to just another failed entrepreneur with no money coming in and precious few prospects. "That was one tough week," Stafford says, shaking his head. "I remember I had to go in and tell all my employees, and that was one of the hardest things to do. They didn't want to hear about what had happened, they only knew about all the great things we had promised them."

Once the initial shock wore off, things only got worse. Stafford could not drum up any new business, and his military retirement payments were being stretched thin just to pay for his Virginia home. Weeks passed, then months, without any change in his dire situation. "I was discouraged," says Stafford. "Now I joke about it and say that I wanted to jump out the window, but my office windows didn't open. But the truth is I was discouraged." Stafford did his best to juggle funds and keep his family afloat. But that meant making hard decisions, and he had to let some bills go unpaid. One day, the lights in his home were turned off, and the Staffords had to make do with candles. Creditors were calling incessantly about overdue accounts—until, that is, Stafford's phones were shut off, too. Then one creditor decided to call his neighbor across the street. "Please tell Mr. Stafford that we called and we need to talk to him about a delinquent account," they told the startled neighbor, much to Stafford's horror. "That may have been the rock-bottom moment," he says. "The lights were off, and then the telephones, and then they call your neighbor to tell them what is going on. I still remember that day as if it was yesterday."

Perhaps most painful of all was not being able to buy Christmas presents for his three young kids. Stafford remembers driving toward Washington, D.C., and having to pull off the Beltway when the reality of his situation finally sank in. Here he was, the promising Earl Stafford, CEO of his own company, earmarked for all kinds of success. And yet, at 41 years old, he didn't have enough money to buy his children Christmas gifts.

"Those things happen" is all that Stafford will say about that depressing drive on the Beltway, as if summoning the emotion he felt is simply too difficult. "You do what you can to survive as a family through times like that."

Driving in his car that night, he felt something he had never felt before. For the first time in his life, Earl Stafford felt like a failure.

He kept driving that difficult night until he pulled into his driveway. His wife was there at home to greet him, and so were his three lovely kids. They had a roof over their heads and they had food to eat. They were still a family, and there was joy in that. "It's a Christian thing, to always take account of the positive things in your life," says Stafford. "I love my wife, I love my kids, I'm not going to the hospital to see sick friends or to the cemetery to bury a loved one. I have the support of my church and my family. Overall, a lot of positive things are happening in my life."

Stafford's refusal to dwell on the negative resulted from one crucial moment early in his crisis. The night in July 1990, when he got the call from RVA and realized both his big contracts were lost, Stafford sat in a chair in his lonely office and had a good conversation with himself. "I was sitting there trying my best to feel sorry for myself, and I remember saying, 'So what are you going to do now, Earl? Are you going to quit?' And very quickly I answered myself: 'No, you're not going to quit, what is wrong with you? You're going to pick yourself up, dust yourself off, and get on with it.'" Stafford would endure many, many moments of anxiety and self-doubt after that conversation, but he made sure never to dwell for too long on his misery. Even in the dark of night, when he couldn't fall asleep for hours, Stafford didn't allow himself to wallow in self-pity. "Even in the darkest moments, I knew deep down that I was going to be all right," he says. "Maybe it's stupidity, but I have always been an optimist in life. And I just knew that it was going to happen for me, sooner or later. I didn't know how, but I just knew. To me, adversity is just the dues you pay to get into the club."

"Do not feel sorry for yourself," Stafford goes on. "Otherwise, you will get wrapped up in all those negative feelings, and then you will fail for sure. Do not dwell on the negative things. Keep on going, keep on pushing, because when you think positive, positive things will happen. You are as you think. Dollars do not equal success—success is a state of mind."

•••

Stafford's conversation with himself set the stage for the next 18 months. He kept pushing, kept up appearances, kept believing in himself—and kept believing in God. "Faith is the one thing that really got me through," he says. "The good Lord knows what He's doing." Stafford got up every day and pored through trade publications, looking for contracts. None of his bids were accepted, and few of his phone calls were returned. Still, he kept bidding, kept calling, kept *going*. Any day now, he told himself, I'm going to turn that corner.

Finally, Stafford heard that NYMA, Inc., the outfit that had brought him aboard the Hubble project, had just secured a contract with the Resolution Trust Corporation, the federal agency in charge of protecting depositors in failed Savings & Loan banks. Stafford bid on a contract to provide consulting, moving, and janitorial services to NYMA. It wasn't a glamorous, high-tech job, but it was a job. Stafford held his breath while his bid was reviewed. In 1991, UNITECH won the job.

Of course, in 1991, UNITECH consisted entirely of Earl Stafford. But that was okay. Stafford attacked his new position with the same gusto he shoveled snow with as a kid back in Jersey. "I would sit in with this systems integration team, and when they left for the day, I would stay and clean up the office, take out the trash, do whatever needed to be done," Stafford says. "I'd get home at 2:00 a.m., kiss my wife and kids, get some sleep, then get up early and do it all again." As great as it felt to be working again, Stafford still had to make do with almost no cash in hand. "It was one of those things where the guys at work say, 'Hey, we're all going out to lunch, you want to join us?' And you say, 'Sorry guys, I'm too busy.' But it's really because you don't have the money to buy yourself lunch."

It wasn't long before Stafford's persistence paid off. The RTC needed bids on a 3-year, $2.5 million subcontract to run computer operations and set up data base systems. But an RTC executive decided against asking for bids on the contract. Instead, he awarded it outright to Earl Stafford. "He knew I worked hard and he knew I had this little company, and he decided to sole-source the contract to me," says Stafford. "I had been up and I had been down and now, again, I was up." This time, things started picking up quickly. Stafford hired employees, developed software, delivered results. Before long, the RTC increased the contract to $5 million—$2 million above the maximum contract amount. "They had to go to the Small Business Administration and get a waiver to go to $5 million!" Stafford recalls with a beaming smile. "That's when things really started happening."

Since that 1992 contract, UNITECH has steadily grown in size and scope. Stafford and his team began developing training software, until they became specialists in multimedia training systems for military agencies and civilian businesses. Today, UNITECH provides software that enables Army troops to conduct virtual training exercises on computers. Soldiers can learn to fix jeeps, drive tanks, and shoot guns simply by sitting at a terminal and booting up one of UNITECH's innovative CD-ROM programs—something known as "distance learning." Stafford's company has also expanded into educational CD-ROMs, and will soon issue a remarkable interactive program that allows high school students to simulate the consequences of taking drugs (several states have already experimented with the technology). In all, UNITECH has contracts in 23 states, employs a staff of some 350, and pulls in revenues of more than $40 million. "We're committed to serving our customers and doing whatever we have to do to get a job done," says Stafford. "I always tell people who work for me, 'With success, there is no elevator to the top floor. You just have to walk.'"

Year after year, UNITECH was acknowledged as one of Virginia's fastest-growing firms. But through it all, Stafford remained unimpressed by such designations. He knew what it was like to grow in a hurry, and he knew that a company could fail just as quickly. Then UNITECH received an SBA Award of Excellence. Standing on stage to accept his award, Stafford was struck by just how far he had come. "That was quite a Kodak moment," he recalls. "But even then I knew not to think more of myself than I should. It's in the Bible that what you give is what you receive, and if you're humble, you are exalted. I have tried to stay humble through it all." To that end, Stafford is involved in several charities, sits on the board of the National Capital Chapter of the American Red Cross and serves as chairman of the Northern Virginia Urban League, among many other civic endeavors. "The thing is, I get really turned on seeing other people succeed," he says. "There are a lot of people out there who need a little help, just like I did at one time."

Stafford's genuine humility is the product of his painful trip to the brink of despair. "I could not be where I am today if all that had not happened," he believes. "Sometimes success can lead to pride and haughtiness. And when you have that early success, maybe you start doing things you shouldn't be doing. Maybe you start smoking dope or something like that. And then your life starts to be controlled by success. I've seen that happen to many people. What happened to me was a real reality check, and while I wouldn't ever want to go through it again, I can honestly say that I'm very glad it happened this way. The Lord only knows what might have become of me otherwise."

"Looking back on that time," he says, "I think it happened for a reason, and that was to make me strong and make me humble. It really is true that if a setback doesn't kill you, it serves to make you stronger."

The ordeal taught Stafford important lessons that are still the core values of his company—stay humble, serve the customer, and never give up on a job. This last tenet—never giving up—is the single most important advice Stafford would give to anyone who stumbles. "Look, this thing is a 100-yard dash, and you cannot quit at 90 yards. If you quit before it's over, you have no chance at winning a medal. You have to cross the finish line, it's as simple as that. Life is pretty simple that way—all you have to do is persevere."

Earl Stafford's company can be reached at www.unitech1.com

TIPS FOR TOUGH TIMES

The Earl Stafford Story

He who has never failed somewhere, that man cannot be great.

Herman Melville

Success, like failure, changes the way we look at the world. Too much success too quickly can make a person cocky and arrogant, and even leave him or her out of touch with reality. Earl Stafford allowed some early success to tempt him into believing he was invincible, and when disaster struck, he got the lesson of his life.

That is why Stafford values the failure he endured almost as much as the success he eventually enjoyed. Failure imbued him with a permanent sense of humility, something he has passed on to his own children. Failure also taught him that, while you can't always control circumstances, you can control your own state of mind. He learned to trust in his faith and his core beliefs, the guideposts that get you through the roughest storms. Nothing builds character quite like a gut-testing setback, and in that sense, Stafford realized, those who experience failure are, indeed, fortunate.

1. **Don't Get Wrapped Up in Negative Feelings** It's easy to feel victimized when the roof caves in, but it's important to

move past those feelings as quickly as you can. The tendency is to wallow in negative thinking, to compound a setback by making it seem worse than it is. Why me? What am I going to do? Maybe I'm just cursed! All of these thoughts are perfectly natural to have. But Stafford didn't dwell on his misfortune for too long, and never let fear or self-doubt affect the upbeat, winning attitude he projected to the world. *Get past the knee-jerk, negative feelings before they wrap you up and stop you from moving forward.*

2. **Setbacks Strengthen—Not Weaken—You** Once again, feeling vulnerable is a natural reaction to failing at something. But the truth is that failure gives you access to resources you never had before. Wisdom, resilience, a confidence that you can endure the worst that life can throw at you—all of these things make you a better, stronger person. Recognizing that isn't easy while the walls are collapsing around you, but even small setbacks and minor failures produce the same positive results. *Allow yourself to feel emboldened by failure, for you have already survived what other people continue to fear.*

3. **Don't Expect Your Journey to Be Easy** Stafford likes to tell his employees that there is no elevator to success; you have to take the stairs. His point is that accomplishing anything of value takes hard work and sacrifice,

and the sooner you realize that, the quicker you'll reach your goal. Strife and struggle are simply the dues you pay; failure and dejection are part of the process, too. Why, then, would anyone give up because of a little adversity? *Chasing a dream is like going to battle; get ready to get bruised and bloodied along the way.*

16 CHASING PERFECTION

The Dan Jansen Story

Whether or not you achieve your goal isn't always the most important thing. Sometimes the effort can be just as rewarding.

Dan Jansen

He knew one thing as he stood on the ice that unforgettable day—his destiny would be determined in the next 90 seconds.

Take a moment, if you will, to imagine the pressure of that. Of sealing your fate forever in the relative blink of an eye. Of earning your legacy in less time than it takes to scramble an egg. Of condensing a lifetime of dreams into a few ticks of the clock. Imagine what it must feel like to stand on the line between who you are and who you yet might be.

Now imagine doing all that *with the whole world watching*.

That was the situation Dan Jansen faced as he toed the starting line at the Vikingskipet skating hall in Lillihammer, Norway. A handsome, strapping fellow from Wisconsin, Jansen was one of the very best speed skaters in the world—if not *the* best. And here he was, at the 1994 Olympics, trying to prove it by winning a gold medal. He had been here before, of course—seven times before. And all seven times he had failed, not only to finish first but to win a medal of any kind. Some of the losses could at least be explained. He was just a green-behind-the-ears 18-year-old kid at his first Olympics, in Sarajevo in 1984. And then, 4 years later in Calgary, when he was the big favorite to win a gold medal in his best race, the 500 meters, tragedy struck on the very day he was set to skate. Only hours before his start time, Jansen found out that his beloved older sister Jane had died of leukemia. Racing with a heavy heart, he slipped and fell in the 500 meters, pain and anguish etched on his face. He fell again in the 1000 meters, the second of his two races. After that, his struggles in the Olympics became a full-fledged monkey on his back. At the 1992 games, in Albertville, France, Jansen—still the top speed skater in non-Olympic competitions—managed to stay on his skates in his races, but finished fourth in the 500 meters and twenty-sixth in the 1000. It didn't help that the media had seized on Jansen's tragic story, never ceasing to remind him of his falls and his sister's death. Clearly, the pressure of winning the gold—in races that allowed no margin for error—was playing tricks on Dan Jansen's mind. "His whole life had been defined by trying to be perfect," says Dr. Jim Loehr, the sports psychologist who began working with Jansen just before Albertville. "He was ensnarled by this notion that he had to be completely perfect or else he was a complete failure. Then you add to that all the baggage that he was carrying; the death of his sister, his previous falls, all of that. I mean, how much more could he be expected to take?"

Well, there was one more thing. The day on which he was scheduled to skate his very last Olympic 500-meter race, in Lillihammer, happened to be the exact 6-year anniversary of his sister Jane's passing. Jansen dug deep and gave the race his best, but slipped again and failed to win a medal. His dream of winning Olympic gold in the 500-meters was, cruelly, over. "After that I was like, 'Why is this happening? Why is this going on?' " remembers the affable and soft-spoken Jansen. "It was this depressing feeling, and I was really hard on myself. I even told my coach that I didn't want to skate in the 1000 meters." Crushed that he had let his fans and family down, Jansen sought out a reporter from his hometown paper and said, poignantly, "Sorry, Milwaukee."

But, really, there was no question that Jansen would skate the 1000 meters, in what would be his very final shot at Olympic glory. True, the 1000 was not his best race, but what else could he do but give it his best shot? Seven races in four Olympic games over 10 years, and here he was, at the starting blocks in Vikingskipet hall, on the very brink of his ultimate fate. "If he falls short, he becomes an example of great tragedy, maybe even labeled one of the great chokers in the sport," says Loehr, who was in Lillihammer for Jansen's eighth and final Olympic race. "If he wins, he becomes this unbelievable hero. And the thing that separates those two things is less than a single second in time. It was just unimaginable pressure."

But then the time to skate arrived, and Jansen could no longer dwell on his difficult past. He eased up to the blocks, crouched into his start position, and took one last deep, cleansing breath. This was it. This was finally it.

The starting gun blasted, echoing through the silent hall. And Dan Jansen began skating, toward his destiny.

●●●

The man who brought unprecedented attention to speed skating might not have even taken up the sport, had his family lived in any other city besides West Allis, Wisconsin. The youngest of a bustling brood of nine children, Jansen simply inherited the convenient family pastime. "My oldest sister was really athletic, but she would always get sick in the wintertime because there were no sports for her to play," says Jansen. "So my parents watched a speed skating meet at a park behind our house, and decided to give her a shot at that." By the time he reached skating age, all of his siblings had tried the sport, and so the closets in the Jansen household were filled with new and used skates. "I played a lot of sports and I was pretty good at baseball and football," Jansen recalls. "But it just so happened that our suburb had the only official 400-meter skating oval in the country. If that rink hadn't been there, I don't know if I would have stuck with speed skating. I might have easily chosen another sport. I guess you could say it was an accident of geography that I stuck with it."

In the beginning, young Dan was hardly a natural on the ice. His father Harry recalled that he had wobbly ankles, and that he had to work extra hard to stay on his feet. But, slowly, Jansen became smitten. "I liked the individual nature of skating," he explains. "Not that there isn't teamwork involved because there certainly is. But when the gun goes off, it's just me out there, and if I don't win, it's my fault. And I always liked the challenge of that." His brother Michael, too, was pretty good on the ice, and the two of them kept skating long after their seven older brothers and sisters had moved on to other hobbies. When Dan was just a lanky teenager, he entered his very first international meet in Europe, against skaters 2 or 3 years older. Jansen not only finished fourth, but he also set a junior world record. "Before that," he says, "I didn't even know there was such a thing as a junior world record."

Soon enough it was plain to see that Jansen was something special. Early on, he realized that to reach the highest levels of his sport, he would have to train year-round, not just in the winter-time. Running, cycling, weight-lifting, rollerblading, sprinting up hills—becoming a world-class skater would require a truly gruel-ing training regimen, and a great deal of sacrifice when it came to his social life. It was not an easy decision to make—at least not until 1980, when Jansen watched the powerful and charismatic speed skater Eric Heiden gobble up a fistful of gold medals at the Olympics in Lake Placid, New York. "When I saw him do that, that really made me think how unbelievable it would be to go to the Olympics," says Jansen. "He was a big reason I leaned toward skating." Jansen chose to focus on the 500 meters, believing him-self to be best suited to the shortest sprint in the sport. "I loved the 500 meters," he says. "I always felt that I lost steam in the 1000 meters. Endurance-wise, I always had a mental block about the 1000. I just preferred the shortest races."

A national champion by age 12, Jansen won a spot on the 1984 Olympic squad at age 18, earning the right to travel across the globe to Sarajevo, Yugoslavia. "Those first Olympics were the purest, most magical Olympics I ever competed in," Jansen says. "Marching with the other athletes, meeting all these great peo-ple—it really was the whole thing you dream about as a kid." The icing on the cake was Jansen's surprise fourth-place finish in the 500 meters, an encouraging sign of good things to come. Returning to the United States, Jansen kicked off perhaps the most illustrious non-Olympic speed skating career ever, winning national and world competitions at an incredible pace. By the time the 1988 Olympics in Calgary, Canada, rolled around, Jansen was clearly one of the very best speed skaters in the world, and a heavy favorite to win the gold medal in the 500 meters. "The week before the games, I won the World Championships in my hometown," says Jansen. "I knew and everyone knew that I was skating really well. And in that week, I felt so good, so confident, I was pretty sure I was going to win the 500 meters. I felt that way right up until the night before the race."

What happened the night before is the saddest and most difficult part of Jansen's amazing story. A year earlier, his cheerful, sensitive sister Jane—third youngest of the kids, after Dan and Mike—had gone in for a routine blood test, and had been diagnosed with leukemia. The mother of three, including a 1-year-old, Jane bravely battled the disease, and continued to delight in her brother Dan's skating successes. "My sister had been doing fairly well, but then right around the time of the Olympics there were complications," says Jansen. "She had to undergo a risky procedure that would be really hard on her liver, but there weren't any other options. The day I left for Calgary, I went to see her and said, basically, 'Hang in there, I love you, and I'll see you when I get back.'"

The Jansen family knew that Jane was taking a turn for the worse. But they never expected that she would slide as quickly as she did. Jansen, his father, and a few of his siblings made the trip to Calgary, where Jansen felt physically terrific, despite his concern for Jane. "I skated great the day before the race, but as I was skating off the ice my dad said to me, 'I have to get back, mom wants me at home, Jane's not doing so well.' So I knew things were pretty serious." Still, Jansen went to bed that night thinking positively and hoping that things might work out well.

Then, at 6:00 a.m. the next morning—the day of the 500-meter race—a friend roused him from sleep and told him he had a phone call. Fear gripped Jansen as he made his way down to the basement of the dorm where he was staying to where the phone lines were. "I was shaking," he recalls. "I knew that something was bad." He picked up the phone and talked to his mother and brother, who told him that Jane's blood pressure was dropping quickly. His sister was far too weak to speak, but perhaps Jansen could say something to her. "So they put the phone to her ear, and I talked to her, and I told her I loved her. And that was that. Once I got off the phone, I went back to my room and I cried for a couple of hours."

Jansen forced himself to get up that morning and start his routine—after all, the biggest race of his life was less than 12 hours away. He had just returned from lunch when he found a slip of paper with a message on it for him. He wanted to pretend it wasn't there, to just go to the rink and slip on his skates and skate a million miles away. But he got on the phone and called home and got the news—his sister Jane had died, only 3 hours after Dan had spoken to her for the final time.

The next few hours were some of the worst hours of Jansen's life. He cried, he hugged his teammates, he tried his best to get into his routine. But he could not stop thinking about his sister Jane. "I even talked to my mom about whether or not I should skate that day," he says. "And she said, 'yeah, you should, you have to give it a try.' And I knew that Jane was so into my skating, she would have hated the idea of me not skating. I felt that, as bad as things seem, what else could I do but skate?"

The American skating squad held an emotional team meeting, and dedicated all the day's races to Jane. Jansen was heartened by his teammate's support, but in the warm-ups before his race he felt weak, distant, out-of-sorts. "Compared to how great I felt on the ice the night before, it was just surreal how I felt out there," he says. "When you're skating well, you feel like you can almost run in your skates, they grip the ice so well. But before the race it felt like the skates weren't even mine. I was wobbly, I couldn't control them. And that hurt my confidence." And in the 500-meter race, the slightest hesitation can doom a skater to fail. Then Jansen got off to a false start, jumping just an instant before the gun sounded. It was a bad sign, since Jansen was known for never false-starting.

When the race officially started, Jansen tried his best to block out all the terrible thoughts in his head. But his body didn't feel right, and he skated sluggishly in the first 100 meters. "I was thinking I had to find some acceleration somewhere, and I was going to try and get it in the first turn," he remembers. "And in the second or third stroke in, my left skate just slipped."

The videotape of the fall is hard to watch. Jansen lost his balance and tried to right himself with his arm. But he fell to the ice and slid into a fellow skater, Japan's Yusushi Kuroiwa. Jansen crashed into nearby safety pads and bounced oddly back to his feet, his arms raising quizzically to the heavens, his face contorting in horror and disbelief, his eyes as big and sad as a wounded dog's. "I was shocked because not only did I not win, but I fell," he says, the emotion of the moment still evident in his voice a dozen years later. "And as bad as it may sound, I was bumming because this was what I trained for all those years, and now it was over and I had fallen. And then you say to yourself, 'I can't feel bad about that, my sister died this morning.' So there were a lot of conflicting emotions, and those feelings didn't go away for months."

In those few seconds, the Dan Jansen saga was born. For 3 days before the 1000-meter race, Jansen did all he could to gather himself and recapture some semblance of normalcy. But, physically and mentally, he wasn't the same man. He got off to a great start, and with only 200 meters to go in the 1000, he was on a world record pace. But then, incredibly, he slipped and fell again. The fleetest and most sure-footed skater in the world had fallen twice in the span of 4 days, failing even to finish the two most important races of his life. "That second fall, who knows?" Jansen says, still puzzled. "It might have been some physical fluke, or it might have been a mental thing. Later, my sports psychologist told me that I wasn't going to allow myself to win that race. There may be something to that." Jansen himself admitted to reporters that he was more concerned about his sister than about the outcome of the 1000. All he wanted to do was get home and be with his family.

Back in Wisconsin, Jansen was deluged with something he didn't want—sympathy. He could understand people feeling bad that Jane had died, but why were they all concentrating on him? "I just didn't want everybody feeling sorry for me," he says. "It was time for me to grieve for my sister, and there was all this sympathy for me. I felt terribly guilty about that." The worst moment may have been during his sister's funeral, when the priest decided to address Jansen directly. "He was right in the middle of his sermon when, boom, all of a sudden, he starts talking to me. And I was like, 'Oh, no, please not this.' At the time, I just couldn't handle all the attention focused on me."

It seemed almost inevitable that Jansen would question the one thing he thought he was sure of—his love for speed skating. Perhaps the best thing for him to do was simply walk away from the ice, and put this sad chapter solidly behind him. "There was a period of sort of not knowing what I wanted to do. I felt tired, and I didn't know if I wanted to go through all that work to get ready for the next Olympics in 4 years." Over the weeks, as his intense hurt lessened, Jansen slowly embraced his passion, accepting too that his failures in Calgary would be the backdrop for every future race. That required a major attitude adjustment on his part. "My perspective really changed after Jane died. I just sort of decided that skating was what I love to do, and what I do best. And I told myself that if I could look back on any race and know in my heart I was prepared and did my absolute best, then that would be good enough for me. I mean, whether or not you achieve your goal isn't always the most important thing. Sometimes the effort can be just as rewarding."

Still, Jansen was a fierce competitor, and deep down he craved the chance to make good on his dreams. "Yeah, I love to win, I wanted to win, and that's how you have to be at that level," he says. "You have to really want to win. And I wanted the gold."

•••

Once again, Jansen dominated world and national competitions, maintaining his status as the best sprint skater on the planet. All told, he won more than 30 World Cup races in his career and some 20 medals at the World Championships. To get ready for the 1992 Olympics in Albertville, France—at which he knew he would be barraged by questions about his sister and his fall—Jansen hired Dr. Jim Loehr, a prominent sports psychologist who works with high-level athletes. "The thing is, Dan knew he was the best in the world, he just wanted some confirmation of that on an Olympic level," says Loehr. "But by Albertville the whole world was completely taken by his story. He was a young man who was thrown into this bizarre situation he never dreamed of, and he was receiving all of this attention from the media he didn't want. He was the guy who was supposed to win the 500 meters, not the guy everybody felt sorry for. And so we had to find a way to get that monkey off his back."

With Loehr's help, Jansen was speaking positively before the Olympics. His confidence was sky high, and physically he'd never felt better. A steady rain in Albertville made the ice a little gritty, hindering his powerful racing style. He didn't focus on the sloppy track, but surely it nagged him somewhere in the back of his mind. Still, he had finished either first or second in every single 500-meter race he had skated that year. Why should this one be any different?

Jansen, the overwhelming favorite to win the gold medal in the 500 meters, skated poorly and finished in fourth place. "I was totally baffled," he says now. "I was really ready for that race. I felt good, I wasn't nervous, I was totally confident. And so afterwards I was pretty much in shock." Jansen had 2 days before he was set to race in the 1000 meters, and he chose to stay away from the ice altogether instead of training, staying in his room and feeling confused. He already had a mental block about the 1000 meters, so things didn't look all that promising for him when race day rolled around. Not surprisingly, his skating was choppy and he finished a dismal twenty-sixth. "I didn't really feel like skating the 1000," he admits. "I was pretty depressed."

By now, the response Dan Jansen elicited had gone from pure sympathy to uncomfortable puzzlement. He was playing out a strange personal drama on a very public stage. With every Olympic failure he picked up more psychological baggage, until his mind was a jumble of doubt and disappointment. Who in the world would have blamed him for hanging up his skates after Albertville and ending the misery once and for all? The deciding factor turned out to be a quirk of scheduling—the next winter Olympics would come in 2, not 4, years. "Even before I left France I talked with my coach Peter Mueller," says Jansen, "and we decided then and there that we were going to give it another go."

• • •

Two things happened between the 1992 Albertville Olympics and the 1994 games in Lillihammer. First, Jansen began working intensely with Dr. Loehr, who helped him make a significant shift in his strategy. Throughout his career, Jansen had convinced himself that he was physically suited for the 500 meters, and conversely lacked the stamina to excel at twice that distance. "He said he was a fast-twitch muscle-fiber person, that he had a sprinter's mentality, and that he only skated the 1000 because it was good for his training," says Loehr. "He really disliked the 1000 because he always felt fatigued toward the end of it. And so he never had a belief that he could succeed."

The problem with that thinking was that it loaded all the pressure on one race—the impossibly demanding 500 meters. "It is a very unforgiving race," says Loehr. "If you make one tiny mistake, you're out. And if you're under extra pressure when you're skating it, then it's very difficult *not* to make a small slip. It put an unbelievable amount of pressure on Dan." With Loehr's help, Jansen split his focus between the 500 *and* the 1000 meters. He taught himself to believe that he could win the longer race. Before he went to sleep every night, he would write "I love the 1000" on a slip of paper. "He had so much depth of talent, I knew he could be as good in the 1000 as he was in the 500," Loehr explains. "And by pushing the 1000 a little more, we could defuse the pressure on the 500. Our thing became that Dan would win not one but two gold medals in Lillihammer."

The other key event in Jansen's life hit closer to home. He and his wife, Robin, whom he had married in 1990, had their first child, a daughter they decided to name Jane, after Jansen's sister. "That changed everything in my life," he says. "Once you have a child, everything else sort of becomes secondary. For me, it was great to be able to come home and get away from skating by playing with Jane. It stopped me from allowing skating to be the all-consuming thought in my head all day long. For sure, it took some of the pressure off of me."

Robin and Jane made the trip to Lillihammer, where once again Jansen felt at the top of his game. It seemed that every time he skated he would shatter another track record. Only 2 weeks before the Olympics, he won the World championships in Calgary, setting a blistering world record in the 500. In practice just before the games he broke the 36-second barrier, an astonishing feat and further proof that Jansen was the best. "All that year I was winning my races by two- and three-tenths of a second, which is really a huge amount of time at that distance," he says. "Going into the Olympics I couldn't have been more prepared and confident." Thanks to his work with Loehr, Jansen felt good about both his races, but deep down he still regarded the shorter sprint as his strong suit. For years, everyone expected him to win a gold medal in the 500 meters, and it seemed almost impossible that he could end his career without winning one. Here was his chance to finally right an inexplicable wrong, and he was primed to end the hex once and for all.

Perhaps his most important task was blocking out the media's attention, no easy thing considering that the 500 meters fell on February 14—the 6-year anniversary of the day his sister Jane died. The symmetry of it tickled reporters, who envisioned their subsequent stories of glory and tidy redemption. Jansen chose not to dwell on the significance of the date. He knew that others would make much of it, but personally he wasn't interested. "All I was thinking about was the race itself," he says. "My skating was as good as it's ever been, and so in my heart I knew that basically I was going to win two golds."

Jansen blasted off the blocks and was cruising smoothly after 100 meters. "I was one of the first skaters to go off that day, so I was thinking that I had to put up a really fast time," he says. "When I got to the last turn I just wanted a little extra acceleration, and maybe I pushed a little too hard."

Those watching the race—including Robin, Jansen's family, and Dr. Loehr—could not believe what they were seeing. On his first stride of the final turn, with the finish line tantalizingly in sight, Jansen briefly lost control beneath his left skate. He tried to regain his balance, and his left hand grazed the ice. "It all happened so quickly," he says. "I slipped and then I tried to recover too quickly, and basically I lost all my speed and momentum out of that turn. You know, the final 300 meters of the race had always been my strong suit, the time when I really turned it on. But this time my hand touched the ice and that was that."

Jansen stayed on his skates and finished the race. His time of 36.3 seconds was, he knew right away, not fast enough to win the gold. His wife, Robin, appeared distraught in the stands, and his coach Peter Mueller tried to hide his disappointment behind dark glasses. Jansen himself was almost philosophical in defeat. "I guess my first reaction was, 'Well, this just isn't meant to be.' But then I got pretty depressed, and I even told Peter I didn't want to skate in the 1000. I mean, as well as I was skating the 1000, the 500 was my *baby*. That was the race I really should have won."

•••

Could it really be ending like this? Could Dan Jansen, the world's best skater at 500 meters, possibly fail to win a gold medal? How could such a nice and decent person be the recipient of so much rotten luck? It was an almost unbearably sad scenario for his fans to contemplate. Just how terrible must Jansen himself have felt about his failure?

In fact, Jansen had a secret weapon to take his mind of the race—his daughter Jane. "After the 500, I went back to the house and I picked her up and I played with her on the floor," Jansen says. "I watched her crawl around and I just thought about how miraculous she was. Having her there with me in Lillihammer was huge. It was such a great distraction, even if it was for only 10 minutes here and there. To be able to play with her and not think about what just happened was great."

No, winning a gold medal was not the most important thing in Jansen's life, not by a long shot. He had spoiled what would have been a storybook ending to his interminable saga, but so what? He was still alive, still healthy, still a father to this precious little 10-month-old child—and he would be no matter what happened in the 1000 meters. And if that didn't lessen the load on his shoulders, nothing would.

The next morning, Jansen gave his little girl a squeeze, then got back to work. "I started getting ready for the 1000 and it was a little awkward," he says. "All the other skaters didn't know what to say to me, they felt sorry for me. Everyone expected me to win, and here I had come up short yet again. So it was very uncomfortable." Jim Loehr knew that the somber mood around Jansen would not lift on its own. "There was a huge history of failure and frustration, and Dan had just added to it," he says. "And I knew that the press would just not let it go. Dan had to figure out a way to deal with it himself." Loehr and Jansen created a small war room, where the skater retreated and reconditioned himself to believe he could win the 1000. "It wasn't going to be easy," Loehr says. "I mean, he had just lost the 500 meters, which was his race. And when an athlete gets hurt badly like that, in such a big event, it's almost unthinkable that he can dedicate himself 100 percent to the next race. But it is a testament to Dan's gutsiness that he did just that."

Ironically, the only way that Jansen could throw himself completely into the 1000 meters was to abandon any expectation of winning. "If anything, I probably even thought, 'Okay, it's not going to happen this time.' I mean, I still believed I could win, but I just didn't *expect* to win anymore." Instead, Jansen decided to do just one thing in his last Olympic race—enjoy it. "Speed skating had been such a wonderful thing in Dan's life, a phenomenal gift to him and his family," says Loehr. "He had learned so many lessons, and had reached such a powerful understanding of life. He had become a stronger human being, and no matter what, skating would always be a wonderful thing for him. And with that in mind, the most important thing became that he enjoy the last Olympic race of his life more than anything he's ever done before. After the race, he should be able to say, 'I was totally at peace with myself, I did the very best that I could, and I enjoyed every single second of the final race of my life.'"

Jansen embraced this new approach, but in the hours before the race the pressure of his situation got to him again. "I felt nervous," he says. "I felt like I didn't want to let people down again." For the first time in his life, he jumped on a stationary bicycle right before the race and sped through two quick sprints to get the blood flowing in his stiffening body. But even so, minutes before start time, he didn't feel right. "I wasn't gripping the ice, I wasn't solid at all. And if you're not gripping the ice you're not going to be able to accelerate like you need to. More than anything I just wanted the race to be over."

But then the gun sounded, and everything changed. "I got to the first turn, and everything was just flowing," Jansen says. "I was totally relaxed, and I just waited in the turns until I reached the apex, and then I would accelerate out of them perfectly. I was getting so much acceleration out of my turns, I could just go smoothly in the straightaways. I mean, I was really cruising." With only three-quarters of a lap to go, Jansen was on a pace to set a new world record—and, more importantly, to win the gold medal that had eluded him for years.

And then Dan Jansen stumbled again.

• • •

Gasps could be heard in the Vikingskipet arena as the hard-luck skater wobbled once more. "It was the second to last turn, and I just sort of slipped a little," Jansen says. "I don't know, I guess it was a mental thing. Sort of like me saying to myself, 'Okay, you can't have it this easy, not after all that.'" Jansen's skate came perilously close to hitting a block on the track, but it just missed and somehow he stayed upright. He lowered a hand to regain his balance, but unlike in the 500 meters 2 years earlier, this time his fingers did not graze the ice. "It all happened in a split second, but I remember thinking when I stumbled that I almost didn't care," Jansen says. "I was like, 'All right, so what, don't try and get it back too quickly, just finish the race.' And so I laid back and took it easy, and I was still able to accelerate out of that turn. The key is I didn't panic."

All of Jansen's mental gymnastics had paid off. All of his efforts to convince himself that he didn't expect to win had, in that split second, allowed him to stay calm and focused. He had lost a few hundredths of a second, but he managed to keep his cool. Jansen breezed across the finish line in 1:12:43 seconds, a new world record. "I knew right away it was a good race," he says. "And I think I knew that it was good enough for some kind of medal."

In the stands his wife Robin hyperventilated with joy. With one lap to go in the final competitor's race, Jansen knew that he had finally won a gold medal. He felt intense relief—not for himself so much as for his family. "I just thought, 'Finally, they can be happy for me.' They had watched all my other Olympic races and expected me to win, and it had never worked out. But now they could go out and celebrate and have fun and cut loose. It was an unbelievable feeling."

Jansen stood proudly on the podium as they played the American national anthem. All he could think of up there was his sister Jane. "I felt that somehow I had to connect with her, and I looked up at the sky and saluted her," Jansen recalls. "I wasn't even aware that I was doing it." After he had been awarded his gold medal, an official grabbed him and told him he had to skate a victory lap. Dan Jansen, the man who had lost seven straight Olympic races that he should have won, didn't know there was such a thing as a victory lap for Olympic gold medalists. "I had to send someone down to get my skates," he laughs.

And then he was on the ice again, skating the most magical lap of his life. With the fans in the stands cheering him wildly, and American flags unfurling dramatically all over the arena, Jansen basked in a moment that many feared might never come. Over the P.A. system, the Norwegian announcer read a stirring poem to Jansen. "I remember your poet, Robert Frost," he intoned. "He said, 'Nothing gold can stay. *But you who knows what it means to have lost, can really stay gold today.*'"

The best, however, was yet to come. Jansen looked into the stands and saw a security guard holding his daughter over the railing. "So I just skated over and picked her up and held her as I went on my victory lap," Jansen says. "And she was waving and laughing and smiling. And then they turned off all the lights and put this big spotlight on us." With flashbulbs popping wildly and flowers littering the ice, Jansen was seized by a most ironic thought: "Well, falling went through my mind again," he admits. "Especially since I was holding Jane." But Dan Jansen did not fall. Not this time.

Next came the customary call from President Clinton. Then there was the huge rally back in Wisconsin. Jansen choked up thanking his parents, "who taught me not only how to win but how to lose." It seemed that an enormous weight had been lifted, not only off of Jansen's back but also off the entire world. "It was just so gratifying to see a story end the way it's supposed to end," says Loehr. "This guy had done everything humanly possible to overcome what happened to him, and that's why it was so easy to root for him. What happened to him wasn't fair, but life isn't fair sometimes. But a gold medal was the right way for his story to end."

Looking back, the victory changed Jansen's outlook on all the failures that had preceded it. "I really learned a lot about myself for all that happened," he says. "I learned that I am a lot stronger than I thought I was." Today the skater is retired and running the Dan Jansen Foundation, which, among other things, raises money for families visiting their ailing children in faraway hospitals. He is also a very successful motivational speaker. But above all, he cherishes the time he spends with his two daughters: Jane, now 7, and little Olivia, who is 4. "They're incredible," he says. "They're not into ice skating yet, but they do like to rollerskate."

Clearly, his children—and not medals—are the greatest prize in Jansen's life. After he won at Lillihammer, he held an impromptu press conference at the airport in Milwaukee. He gave a stirring speech to a delirious crowd of 1000, which went absolutely wild when he showed them his gold medal. Then Jansen took his daughter Jane in one hand and an American flag in the other, and walked happily away from the podium, grinning from ear to ear. In the heat of the moment, he left something behind at the podium.

Dan Jansen forgot his gold medal.

TIPS FOR TOUGH TIMES

The Dan Jansen Story

A minute's success pays the failure of years .
                                        Robert Browning

*F*ew athletes have ever experienced the pressure of failure *quite as intently as Dan Jansen. With each successive defeat in an Olympic race, it became harder and harder not to fixate on his flaws. Perhaps his greatest accomplishment was sustaining the positive attitude he needed to finally accomplish his goal of winning an Olympic gold medal—a truly remarkable feat given the scrutiny his performances drew.*

In essence, Jansen is an expert on how to respond to failure. One way, of course, is to just give up, to believe that you are somehow cursed by the gods. Another is to wipe the slate clean every time you try again. This was not an easy thing for Jansen to do; in fact, his Olympic career was all but over before he finally accomplished it. But once he did, he became a testament to the incredible will to win that resides in all of us, to the indestructibility of the human spirit.

1. **Don't Be Afraid to Tweak Your Goals** For years, Jansen devoted himself exclusively to the 500 meters, the most demanding of all the speed-skate races. By allowing

himself so little margin of error, he boxed himself into a corner that required utter perfection to escape. It was only when he shifted his focus to also encompass the 1000-meter race that he finally took enough pressure off himself to win the gold medal he coveted. *Be unyielding in pursuit of your goals, but don't be obstinate when it comes to adjusting them; subtle shifts of focus can produce amazing results.*

2. **Don't Let Past Failures Become Baggage** Each of Dan Jansen's races was inevitably linked to his previous failures, and especially to the tragic fall in the race that followed his sister's death. But that link was far more vivid for the media than it ever was for Jansen. He correctly grasped the true definition of failure. Missing out on medals didn't mean that he had failed; allowing the fear of falling again to prevent him from racing would have been the true failure. Giving it another go can never be construed as failure, and so each new race was a fresh shot at glory for Jansen. In some ways he succeeded by merely persevering; it meant that he had not succumbed to the inhuman pressure he faced. *Failure is not coming up short, it's allowing the fear of coming up short that will stop you from trying in the first place.*

3. **Abandon the Expectation to Win** Athletes are always urged to think of themselves as winners, to visualize victory and

settle for nothing less. But in many cases the expectation of winning can inhibit performance. Certainly in Jansen's case, 10 years worth of expectations had produced a crippling level of pressure. Finally, before his last race, Jansen deflated those expectations by telling himself he no longer expected to win the gold. Instead, he made it his goal to have as much fun in his last Olympic race as he could. The strategy paid off, and Jansen skated the smoothest, most relaxed race of his life. *Achieving your goal should be your main focus, but not always your sole focus; sometimes taking the pressure off is just what's needed.*

About the Author

Alex Tresniowski is a senior writer for *PEOPLE* magazine, where his features include cover stories on Paul McCartney, Kate Moss, Tiger Woods, and many others. Beyond his coverage of celebrities, Tresniowski writes about a wide variety of ordinary people who do extraordinary things; he has also written articles for *Time*, *Instyle*, and *Teen People*. Tresniowski is the author of the critically praised *The Book of Twins*, and has appeared on such popular TV shows as *Access Hollywood* and *Entertainment Tonight*. He lives in New York City.